THREE VEG AND MEAT

FLIP THE BALANCE ON YOUR PLATE

OLIVIA ANDREWS

MURDOCH BOOKS

SYDNEY · LONDON

CONTENTS

WELCOME TO A NEW WAY OF EATING

Once upon a time I didn't really care about eating a healthy, balanced diet. I just loved food, in all its wonderful forms. If I liked the look of something, I would just eat it, without a second thought about what it was doing to my body, let alone the planet.

Our childhood memories and experiences often shape the way we eat. As a child, I was regularly fed snack foods, almost as a staple, and I know that this is why I still crave them as an adult. Every day in primary school I had a packet of chips for morning tea, and often a small white-bread sandwich, usually smeared with margarine and topped with 'plastic' cheese. To this day these are two of my guilty pleasures — except I've replaced the margarine with butter in the sandwich, and I fry it all in a pan until the cheese melts! After that lunch though, Mum usually made us lovely home-cooked meals for dinner, and we always sat around the table to eat them. We never had dessert, so I find I have little interest in sweets as an adult, and only very rarely do I make dessert at home.

Early on in my career I was writing recipes based purely on the look and taste of the food, without much of a social conscience. But, as with most things in life, you learn with age.

A 'REAL FOOD' REVELATION

In 2015 at a Swedish primary school in Malmo I witnessed something extraordinary: children being fed 'real food' — vegetables and legumes, fish and meat, flavoured with spices and herbs — 'normal' healthy food that adults would eat, and not a separate, dumbed-down menu full of processed, unidentifiable things.

The children were featuring on the TV show *Destination Flavour Scandinavia*, and the food memories and positive associations being established would ensure good eating habits carried through to adulthood. And all this was done in a sustainable way, with an emphasis on totally organic ingredients.

Would this ever be possible to achieve in other countries, I wondered.

One year later, I gave birth to my daughter, Harriet. Wanting to give her the best possible start in life, I was determined not to expose her to some of the junk that is seen on kids' menus, and I did my best to give her an improved version of most foods. She is my greatest inspiraton and motivation for writing this book.

Since starting up the culinary department at Marley Spoon Australia (a company that delivers fresh meal-kits to homes) in 2015, I've also learned a lot about the flavours Australians enjoy and what they *really* want to eat, especially on weeknights.

As a recipe writer, I've become increasingly interested in creating more nutritionally balanced recipes for people to enjoy at home every day. What do we really need to consume for our bodies to receive the right amount of nutrients? What does 'balance' actually mean?

MEET 'THREE VEG AND MEAT'

For all our lives the majority of us have been told that red meat is the source of iron, dairy is the source of calcium, and that we must eat meat, meat and more meat to satisfy our bodies' desperate need for protein. But health authorities are now saying that most of us consume an over-abundance of animal-based products and that instead our diets should be made up of 70 per cent plant-based foods, and that vegetables should fill up 50 per cent of every plate we eat.

There is a wealth of evidence that eating plenty of vegetables can help us maintain a healthy body weight, lower cholesterol and blood pressure, and protect us against chronic diseases such as type 2 diabetes, heart disease, stroke and certain cancers. A diet rich in fruits vegetables and wholegrains can also reduce the risk of depression and improve overall mood and wellbeing, as well as memory and learning.

Alarmingly, the average Australian adult only eats about half the amount of vegetables they should — and the vast majority of children aren't consuming enough vegetables each day. This situation is pretty similar in the United Kingdom and United States.

Plant-based foods are what our bodies need, and what most of us are lacking. Our plates should be 50 per cent vegetables and our diets 70 per cent plant-based foods.

WHAT SHOULD WE REALLY BE EATING?

The chart below shows the number of serves the Australian Dietary Guidelines recommend we eat every day from each of the five core food groups for a nutritious and balanced diet.

If you are pregnant or breastfeeding, see: www.nutritionaustralia.org/national/resource/ australian-dietary-guidelines-recommended- daily-intakes

AGE GROUP	DAILY SERVES VEGETABLES & LEGUMES	DAILY SERVES FRUIT	DAILY SERVES GRAINS (CEREAL)	DAILY SERVES LEAN MEAT, POULTRY, FISH, EGGS, NUTS, SEEDS	DAILY SERVES MILK, YOGHURT, CHEESE
1–8 years	2–4½	½–1½	4	1–1½	1–1½
9–18 years	5–5½	2	4–7	2½	2½–3½
19–70 years	5–6	2	4–6	2–3	2½–4
70+ years	5–6	2	3–4½	2–2½	3½–4

LET'S HIT THE RESET BUTTON

This book is designed to flip the balance of our meals, pushing the meat to one side of the plate and making vegetables the star — ramping up all the nutritional benefits of eating plenty of vegetables, without compromising on flavour, taste and texture.

The best 'diet' in life is a sustainable one. For me personally, becoming vegetarian or vegan, or abstaining from certain food groups

for extended periods, always backfires, and I tend to over-compensate for any 'sacrifices' by bingeing — making up for lost time. And sometimes, if you crave a certain food, chances are your body needs it.

By putting more of the right 'stuff' on our plates, we are doing so much better by our health, our weekly budget and the planet, while also contributing to a more sustainable way of life.

FROM VEGAN TO FLEXITARIAN: SOMETHING FOR EVERYONE

In this book you can expect to find your favourite dishes and 'junk food' classics, reimagined. There is something for everyone, whether you are vegan, vegetarian, pescatarian, an omnivore, or prefer to eat dairy or gluten free. And if your household contains a mixture of all these eating styles, you will find plenty of solutions for your family, with a huge variety of base recipes that you can easily adapt for vegetarians and even vegans.

More than 50 per cent of the recipes are either vegan, or vegan-able (able to be adapted for vegans). About 70 per cent of the recipes are dairy free, or offer dairy-free alternatives, while about 65 per cent of the dishes are gluten free or gluten-freeable (able to be made gluten free).

WHEN LESS IS MORE

I like to know where my food comes from, which is why I buy good-quality meat whenever possible, be it free range, organic or grass fed. When it comes to chicken and eggs, I only buy organic. This is the trade off: I prefer to eat less of these items and buy only the best quality. We might be able to buy cheap meat that comes from factory farms, but is that what we want to be eating? This is why I enjoy dairy in moderation too.

The meat recipes in this book use a smaller quantity than the 150–200 g (5½–7 oz) per serve of animal protein that many of us are accustomed to, but I have also included plant-based protein sources whenever possible. The size of one serve of meat should be comparable to a pack of cards.

NUTRITION AT A GLANCE

The primary message of this book is to eat more plant-based foods in the form of vegetables, so I offer different solutions for how you can do this. Every recipe has a nutrition circle showing how many serves of vegetables it contains (see the chart on page 5). Under each recipe you'll also find notes highlighting other nutritional benefits — whether it's high in a particular vitamin or mineral, or low in saturated fat (2 g or less) or cholesterol (20 mg or less) — as opposed to counting calories only. Having said that, the recipes in the chapter 'Keeping it Light' average 450 calories per serve, and those in the 'Dinner Time' chapter average 650 calories per serve.

Also note that where a recipe serves 4–6, the nutritional analysis has been averaged out based on 5 serves, rather than 4 or 6.

I have written the recipes to make it very easy to obtain your five daily serves of veg — remembering that breakfast and lunch are also opportunities to consume some vegies, not just dinner time. It is always good to be aware of what you have eaten throughout the day so that you can balance out your daily diet overall and ensure you are consuming enough of everything else you need, too.

In this book, you can expect to find your favourite dishes and 'junk food' classics, reimagined. There is something for everyone, whether you are vegan, vegetarian, pescatarian, an omnivore, or prefer to eat dairy or gluten free.

WISDOM OF THE FRENCH

I think it would be even better if we could adopt the French way of eating. In France the main meal of the day is lunch (when you most need the energy), followed by a much lighter dinner. I find this approach keeps my weight in check, and I sleep much better too. I realise this isn't practical for many people, especially those who rarely get a decent lunch break. Still, the more time our food has to digest properly, the better. For this reason, I prefer to eat a light dinner with my daughter around 5–6 pm.

Check out my meal plans on the next few pages for lighter and larger meal options. (Oh, and the French don't believe in separate kids' menus either!)

SCALE IT BACK A BIT

I came from a family where second helpings of dinner (and sometimes thirds!) was normal. I'd eat until I was bursting — partly because I loved eating, but also because I thought that was the thing to do: eat until you were full. If I wasn't full, I wasn't satisfied. I still struggle with this today, and it has certainly been a contributing factor to weight issues throughout my life. The Chinese say we should stop eating when we are nearly three-quarters full. I may have Chinese heritage, but sadly that valuable advice didn't filter through to me!

Over the decades, our waistlines have been expanding, and even the physical size of our plates has grown. The more food you serve your family, the more likely it is that they will eat it all, which might be more than they actually need. If this sounds like your family, using smaller plates is a great idea.

BREAKING IT ALL DOWN

How often have you eaten a slice of cake or quiche and really thought about the ingredients that went into it — how many eggs, how much flour, butter or sugar? It's very easy not to think about it when it tastes so good. This is something I've considered very carefully in this book. I wanted to ensure the ingredients (and quantities) in the various recipes are nutritious, so you can feel confident that you're not blowing out on the nutrition and calorie scales, and that you're getting your five serves of veg a day — often by unexpected means!

The recipes in this book also use minimal dairy. I know most things taste better with butter or cheese, but if I am going to use dairy, I'd rather use just enough of the real thing to retain the character of a dish. I never recommend hydrogenated oils, such as

margarine, as they contain nasty trans fats. The vegan shortcrust pastry on page 204 contains no dairy at all, and it works so well and tastes so good that I even suggest using it in recipes that contain meat.

Similarly, I have tried to use as little sugar as possible, particularly in the desserts, drawing instead upon the natural sweetness of fruit and vegetables. Yes, you'll find the odd teaspoon of sugar (in various forms), because I feel it's important to balance flavours within a dish, but it's never excessive and you will know exactly how much you're putting in.

I also recommend seasoning food throughout the cooking process. Of course, we need to be really careful with children, because their little kidneys can't process a lot of salt, but when cooking for your family you can control how much salt a meal contains. Seasoning your food with a pinch here and there, from the beginning of the cooking process, helps to unlock the flavours of your ingredients and is minimal compared to the high sodium levels of processed foods, especially in many kids' foods.

EMBRACING FLEXITARIANISM

There is so much to consider when we are feeding ourselves, let alone several other bodies too. It's a big job! And I realise that preparing more vegetables can equal more work in the kitchen, but please don't be put off. Think of it as an investment in your family's wellbeing, both short and long term.

As Michael Pollan, author of *The Omnivore's Dilemma*, wisely says:

'Eat food. Not too much. Mostly plants.'

Can it really be as simple as this? Yes it can.

Eating a 'rainbow' of vegetables each day doesn't have to be tedious. Junk food might be fun, but healthy alternatives to all of our favourites can be fun too! Once you get started, I hope that you enjoy and see value in this new approach to cooking and eating.

WEEKLY MEAL PLANS

During a busy working week, coming up with ideas to feed everyone for dinner each night can sometimes feel daunting.

But with a bit of forward planning, it's quite easy to dish up a varied menu of tasty, vegie-packed weeknight meals that will not only keep the whole family healthy and happy, but save you a lot of shopping, preparation and thinking time too. It will also minimise food wastage, which saves you money too.

Sure, you'll need to do a little preparation at the weekend, but when you have a bit of time, use the opportunity to make extra to freeze for later. That way you can pull a delicious home-cooked meal straight out of the freezer on a night when things haven't gone to plan and you've ended up time-starved and hungry.

So, here are some simple midweek menu ideas to get you started. I've added variations to the recipes to give you as many shortcuts as possible.

Not all of the weekend preparation I've suggested in these meal plans is absolutely necessary, and you can get away with using store-bought passata and stock if you're really squeezed for time. But for the best results and flavour, it's good to make your own whenever you can.

You definitely do need to make the White sauce on page 193 for its many health benefits. I'd also encourage you to make the yoghurt-based Sour-ish cream on page 192, as it's so much healthier than regular sour cream — and so easy to prepare.

LIGHTER MEALS

WEEK 1 AVERAGE 3½ SERVES OF VEG PER MEAL

SATURDAY OR SUNDAY	MONDAY	TUESDAY	WEDNESDAY	THURSDAY	FRIDAY
Make 1½ batches of Roasted tomato passata (page 207) + 2 batches of gravy of your choice (pages 217, 221, 223, 225), reserving ½ quantity for Tuesday, and freezing 1 batch for Week 2 and the remaining ½ quantity for Week 3. Make 1½ batches of White sauce (page 193) and freeze what you don't need for Monday and Tuesday (reserve the leftover cauliflower for Nice fried rice).	Faux cheese ravioli (page 66) + 700 ml Roasted tomato passata + 1 cup (250 ml) White sauce	Poutine (page 93) + ½ quantity gravy of your choice + 600 ml White sauce	Nice fried rice (page 69), using leftover cauliflower from White sauce	Mix-it-up minestrone (page 70)	Warm salmon niçoise (page 65)

WEEK 2 AVERAGE 3 SERVES OF VEG PER MEAL

SATURDAY OR SUNDAY	MONDAY	TUESDAY	WEDNESDAY	THURSDAY	FRIDAY
Buy fish for Monday and make Fish patties (page 230). Make a batch of Bolognese sauce (lamb and/or beef, page 210) and freeze half for Week 3.	Fish bowl (page 78) + thaw gravy overnight in the fridge	Ain't-got-no-beef steaks, mash and gravy (page 90) + thawed gravy	Top cobb salad (page 54)	 Corn and chicken soup (page 57)	Sloppy joes (page 77), using store-bought buns

WEEK 3 AVERAGE 2½ SERVES OF VEG PER MEAL

SATURDAY OR SUNDAY	MONDAY	TUESDAY	WEDNESDAY	THURSDAY	FRIDAY
Make Gnocchi tray bake (optional time saver, page 85)	Gnocchi tray bake (pre-made, with 700 ml Roasted tomato passata)	 Warm salmon niçoise (page 65)	Mix-it-up minestrone (page 70) or Sloppy joes (page 77)	Top cobb salad (page 54)	 Nice fried rice (page 69), using leftover cauliflower from White sauce

WEEK 4 AVERAGE 3½ SERVES OF VEG PER MEAL

SATURDAY OR SUNDAY	MONDAY	TUESDAY	WEDNESDAY	THURSDAY	FRIDAY
Make Chunky tomato ketchup (page 226) + Gnocchi tray bake (optional time saver, page 85)	 Black pepper tofu and prawns (page 89)	Gnocchi tray bake (pre-made with 700 ml tomato passata) + thawed White sauce	 Poutine (page 93) + ½ quantity gravy of your choice + thawed White sauce	 Shout louder for this chowder (page 73)	 'Steak' sandwich (page 86)

DINNERS

WEEK 1 AVERAGE 3½ SERVES OF VEG PER MEAL

SATURDAY OR SUNDAY	MONDAY	TUESDAY	WEDNESDAY	THURSDAY	FRIDAY
Make Sour-ish cream (page 192) + 1½ batches of Roasted tomato passata (page 207). Make and freeze the vego balls on page 227 if you have time.	 Mushroom stroganoff with beef (page 110) + 1 cup Sour-ish cream + 400 ml Roasted tomato passata	 Upside-down chicken kiev (page 132)	Nice fried rice (page 69), using leftover cauliflower from White sauce	Tasty taco salad (page 113), made with beef or prawns + Sour-ish cream	Mega meatball subs (page 136), using the vego balls + 400 ml Roasted tomato passata

WEEK 2 AVERAGE 3 SERVES OF VEG PER MEAL

SATURDAY OR SUNDAY	MONDAY	TUESDAY	WEDNESDAY	THURSDAY	FRIDAY
Make Chunky tomato ketchup (page 226). Buy fish for Monday and make Fish balls for the laksa (page 148), or use prawns in the laksa instead.	Fish ball laksa (page 148)	 Roasted tomato risotto (page 109), using 400 ml Roasted tomato passata	 Buffalo hot things (page 105)	The burger (page 155), using store-bought buns	 Chick chick cacciatore (page 114), using 400 ml Roasted tomato passata

WEEK 3 AVERAGE 6 SERVES OF VEG PER MEAL

SATURDAY OR SUNDAY	MONDAY	TUESDAY	WEDNESDAY	THURSDAY	FRIDAY
Make a double batch of Bolognese sauce (lamb and/or beef) on page 210 and freeze half for Week 4. Make a double batch of White sauce (page 193) and freeze what you don't need for Monday and Tuesday; you could reserve ¾ cup (185 g) of White sauce for Finger-lickin' fish fingers (page 128) or Faux cheese ravioli (page 66) or Poutine (page 93) in Lighter meals meal plans + reserve remaining cauliflower for That's some satay curry (page 106).	 Dreamy not-so-creamy chicken pasta (page 127)	Shepherd's moussaka (page 156), using thawed bolognese sauce	Whiz-bang falafel (page 58)	That's some satay curry (page 106)	Finger-lickin' fish fingers (page 128), made with or without White sauce

WEEK 4 AVERAGE 3 SERVES OF VEG PER MEAL

SATURDAY OR SUNDAY	MONDAY	TUESDAY	WEDNESDAY	THURSDAY	FRIDAY
Make pulled pork for the tacos on page 102 + ½ quantity Sour-ish cream (page 192).	 Pullin' pork tacos (page 102), using the pulled pork + 400 ml Roasted tomato passata	Butter-nut chicken (page 101), using ¾ cup (185 g) Sour-ish cream + 400 ml passata. Thaw bolognese sauce in fridge	 Spaghetti with tomato passata or the thawed Bolognese sauce	 Three-veg medley with fish (page 144)	 Fit-for-an-army eggplant parmi (page 159), using 400 ml Roasted tomato passata

CHAPTER ONE

SNACKS

CLOUD NINE CORN FRITTERS Makes 12 | Serves 4

Everyone loves corn fritters, but nobody loves stodgy ones. These fritters are just right, being loaded with veg, which gives them a wonderful texture. The best bit? You can enjoy them any time of day.

almost
4
SERVES VEG
per serve

500 g (1 lb 2 oz) starchy/floury
  potatoes, peeled

1¾ cups (400 g) Creamed corn
  (page 213)

1¼ cups (250 g) fresh corn kernels,
  or thawed frozen corn kernels

2 eggs, lightly beaten

2 spring onions (scallions), thinly sliced
  (optional)

4 tablespoons wholemeal self-raising
  flour

4 tablespoons cornflour

olive oil, for pan-frying

mixed salad leaves, to serve

Chunky tomato ketchup (page 226)
  or your favourite chutney, to serve

Preheat the oven to 120°C (235°F).

Grate the potatoes into a large bowl. (Alternatively, coarsely chop the potatoes, then process in a blender or food processor until very finely chopped, then transfer the chopped potato and any liquid to a large bowl.)

Stir in the creamed corn, corn kernels, beaten eggs and spring onion, if using, until combined. Fold in the flour and cornflour until just combined and season well with sea salt and freshly ground black pepper.

Pour enough oil into a large frying pan to lightly cover the base. Place over medium heat until the oil is hot. Working in batches, and using 4 tablespoons (⅓ cup) of the batter for each fritter, cook the fritters for 3 minutes on each side, or until golden and cooked through. Drain on paper towel and keep warm in the oven while cooking the remaining fritters.

Serve the fritters warm, with salad leaves and chunky tomato ketchup.

TOP TIPS

- To make the fritters dairy free, use olive oil instead of butter when making the Creamed corn.
- For gluten-free fritters, use gluten-free flour and cornflour.

HEALTHY FATS

+
½ serve wholegrains per serve

MAKE AHEAD
Cooked fritters will keep in an airtight container in the fridge for up to 3 days. Alternatively, wrap them well and freeze for up to 3 months. Gently reheat in the oven or in a frying pan.

THE PERFECT BRUNCH MUFFIN

Makes 12 regular muffins, or 6 giant Texas muffins

These savoury muffins make a tasty brunch or even an afternoon tea snack. They're really great in lunchboxes too. To keep things interesting, try using sweet potato instead of pumpkin, and goat's cheese instead of feta.

almost
1/2
SERVE VEG
per regular
muffin

4 eggs

4 tablespoons extra virgin olive oil

1 zucchini (courgette), coarsely grated; you'll need about 1⅓ cups (180 g)

1⅔ cups (200 g) finely grated peeled pumpkin

2¼ cups (100 g) baby English spinach, finely chopped (in a food processor or by hand)

1 tablespoon lemon thyme or regular thyme leaves

1 teaspoon sea salt

⅔ cup (100 g) of your favourite feta cheese, crumbled

2 cups (300 g) spelt or wholemeal plain flour (or a combination)

3 teaspoons baking powder

Preheat the oven to 180°C (350°F). Grease and line a 6-hole giant Texas or 12-hole standard muffin tin.

Using a fork, lightly beat the eggs and oil in a large bowl. Add the zucchini, pumpkin, spinach, thyme and sea salt and mix until well combined. Fold in the feta, then fold in the flour and baking powder until just combined.

Evenly divide the mixture among the muffin holes.

Bake for 20 minutes, or until the muffin tops are lightly golden, and a skewer inserted into a muffin comes out clean (even if it's slightly sticky); you don't want the muffins ending up too dry.

Remove from the oven and set aside to cool for 10 minutes, before turning out of the tin to serve warm. Alternatively, you can let the muffins cool completely, then store in an airtight container.

TOP TIP

- **Instead of fresh thyme, you could use 2 teaspoons dried mixed Italian herbs, or a similar dried herb blend.**

✚
No added sugars

MAKE AHEAD

The muffins will keep in an airtight container in the fridge for up to 5 days; gently warm in the microwave before serving. They also store well in the freezer for up to 3 months, in an airtight container, or individually wrapped; thaw in the fridge overnight.

JALAPEÑO POPPERS Makes 12 | Serves 6

Easy to prepare in advance, these little beauties aren't quite like the usual deep-fried version stuffed with cheese, but more like the stuffed peppers at the deli counter — although you'll still find it difficult to stop popping them into your mouth. The amount of Sour-ish cream you'll need will depend on the size of your chillies.

1/2 SERVE VEG per serve

12 fat fresh jalapeño chillies
extra virgin olive oil, for drizzling
½ cup (75 g) nuts and seeds, such as
   almonds, pistachios, sunflower and
   sesame seeds, toasted
1½–2 cups (400–550 g) Sour-ish cream
   (page 192)

Preheat the oven to 220°C (425°F). Line a baking tray with baking paper.

Place the chillies on the baking tray, drizzle with oil, season with salt and toss to coat. Spread them out in a single layer and roast them on the highest shelf of the oven for 8–10 minutes, or until the skins have blistered and split.

Meanwhile, finely chop the toasted nuts or seeds, or pulse in a food processor, until they have a crumb-like consistency. Set aside.

When the chillies have finished roasting, carefully transfer them to a bowl. Cover with a plate and set aside to steam, to help release the skin from the flesh. When cool enough to handle, peel off and discard the skins. Using a sharp knife, carefully cut around the top of each and gently pull out the stem and seeds.

Fill each chilli with the sour-ish cream; don't worry if some of it ends up on the outside. Roll each chilli in the nut mixture to coat and serve.

TOP TIP
• You can finely chop the nuts by hand, but a food processor gives you a better crumb-like texture, which coats the chillies more easily and evenly.

LOW CARB

Over 150% RDI vitamin C per serve
(mostly from chillies)

MAKE AHEAD
You can bake and stuff the chillies up to 3 days ahead and leave them uncoated, but once you roll them in the nuts they won't keep as well. You can also crush the nuts up to 3 days ahead; just roll the chillies in the nut mixture when ready to serve.

EVERYBODY LOVES DUMPLINGS Makes about 40 | Serves 8

I'm not sure I've ever met anyone who doesn't like a dumpling. The beauty of making them at home is that you can stuff them with whatever you like, to suit your tastes. This method describes the easiest way to make a dumpling. Depending on how you'd like to present them, you can buy square or round wrappers, and also pleat or gather up the wrapper in the middle of the dumplings.

almost 1/2 SERVE VEG per serve

275 g (10 oz) packet of wonton
   or gow gee wrappers
1 quantity Pork dumpling balls mixture
   (page 233)
grapeseed or rice bran oil, for
   pan-frying (optional)
soy sauce, to serve
Chinese black vinegar, to serve
Sesame salt (page 200), to serve
   (optional)

If steaming your dumplings, fill a saucepan or wok with 5 cm (2 inches) water and place a lightly greased steamer on top. Alternatively, you can line the steamer with baking paper, and use a fork to prick holes in the paper to let the steam escape. Bring the water to a simmer.

Meanwhile, half-fill a small bowl with water. Working in batches, lay out up to eight dumpling wrappers on a clean work surface. Put 2 heaped teaspoons of the pork mixture into the centre of each. Dip a fingertip into the bowl of water and moisten the pastry borders. Fold over to enclose the filling, ensuring there are no air pockets, and press the edges well to seal. If you want to make 'pot sticker' dumplings, gently flatten the base.

Very carefully add the dumplings to the steamer, put the lid on and steam for 10 minutes, or until cooked through.

Alternatively, working in batches, heat 1 tablespoon oil at a time in a large frying pan over medium heat. Add a batch of dumplings and cook for 2 minutes, or until the base is golden. Pour in ½ cup (125 ml) water and cover with a lid, then cook for a further 6–8 minutes, or until the dumplings are cooked through and the water has evaporated. You may need to add a little extra water, depending on your pan; if so, just add ¼ cup (60 ml) water at a time. Keep each batch in a warm place in a covered container while cooking the remaining dumplings.

In a small bowl, combine equal quantities of soy sauce and black vinegar, to make a dipping sauce.

Serve the dumplings hot, with the dipping sauce and sesame salt, if desired.

DIVIDE AND CONQUER
• Make half the dumplings vegan. Make the pork mixture on page 233, but using only half the amount of pork, and leaving the pork out of the base mixture for the moment. Divide the base mixture between two bowls. To one bowl, add 125 g (4½ oz) finely chopped shiitake or wood ear mushrooms (either fresh or rehydrated), or crumbled firm tofu. To the other bowl, add the pork. Shape the dumplings as directed, cooking the vegan batch first.

LOW SATURATED FAT

• ½ serve protein per serve
• No added sugars

MAKE AHEAD
Freeze uncooked dumplings in an airtight container for up to 3 months, keeping them separate between pieces of baking paper. To cook them, leave them on the bench while your steamer comes up to a boil, then steam for 15 minutes, or until cooked through.

PESCATARIAN • VEGAN-ABLE • DAIRY FREE • GLUTEN FREE • NUT FREE • EGG FREE

SUSHI CAKE Serves 6–8

This impressive party number looks quite elaborate, but is actually much easier and quicker to assemble than individual sushi rolls, and is simply cut into wedges for serving. For a vegan sushi cake, simply omit all the seafood — or make one side pescatarian and the other vegan or vegetarian. Experiment by substituting seaweed salad, seasoned tofu, grated beetroot or even thinly sliced blanched green beans for some of the ingredients.

just under
1
SERVE VEG
per serve

2 cups (420 g) sushi rice

⅓ cup (60 g) red or black quinoa, rinsed well

4 tablespoons rice vinegar, plus an extra for the water bowl

1 tablespoon raw sugar

1 teaspoon fine sea salt

6–8 sheets toasted nori seaweed

125 g (4½ oz) tin good-quality mackerel or tuna, drained

1½ tablespoons Mayo (page 192); optional

200 g (7 oz) peeled cooked prawns

1 carrot, finely grated

1 ripe avocado, halved, thinly sliced lengthways

1 large Lebanese cucumber, thinly sliced lengthways, or peeled into strips

100 g (3½ oz) sliced cured trout or salmon

To serve
pickled ginger
gluten-free soy sauce
wasabi

Wash the rice and quinoa in a fine sieve under cold running water until the water runs clear. Place in a saucepan with 600 ml (21 fl oz) water. Cover with a lid and bring to a simmer over medium heat, then immediately reduce the heat to low and cook for 12 minutes, or until the water has been absorbed. Turn off the heat. Stand, covered, for 10 minutes.

Meanwhile, combine the vinegar, sugar and salt in a small saucepan over low heat, stirring until the sugar and salt have dissolved. Cool to room temperature.

Cut the nori sheets to fit three layers of a round 20 cm (8 inch) spring-form cake tin, then set the sheets aside. Line the tin with 4–5 layers of plastic wrap, to allow for easy removal of the sushi cake.

Add a dash of extra vinegar to a small bowl of water, to use as a finger bowl.

Transfer the rice mixture to a large container or bowl. Slowly and evenly drizzle the cooled vinegar brine over the rice and mix with a rice paddle, thin spatula or wooden spoon until the grains are well coated, using a gentle cutting motion. Constantly fan the mixture to cool it down to room temperature; a plastic lid is great for this.

Break up the mackerel in a bowl and combine with the mayo, if using. Reserve five prawns as a garnish, cut the rest in half lengthways and set aside.

Evenly press one-third (about 2 cups) of the rice mixture onto the base of the cake tin, dipping your fingertips into the bowl of vinegar water to stop the rice sticking to your fingers. Place a nori layer on top. Arrange all the sliced prawns in an even layer over the nori, then cover with all the carrot, filling in any gaps.

Evenly press another one-third of the rice mixture into the tin. Top with a nori layer, then spread all the mackerel mixture over. Alternate the next layer with most of the avocado and cucumber slices, reserving a few slices of each to garnish.

Finish with a final layer of rice, then nori. Drape the surface with the sliced trout. Top with the reserved whole prawns, avocado and cucumber.

Cut into wedges and serve with pickled ginger, soy sauce and wasabi.

The sushi cake is best served straight away, but can also be assembled a few hours ahead and refrigerated.

TOP TIP

- You can also use a square 20 cm (8 inch) loaf (bar) tin, but the sushi cake won't be as easy to remove and will be quite heavy. Line the tin with a few layers of plastic wrap to help lift the cake out.

LOW SATURATED FAT

½ serve protein per serve

FRENCH ONION COB DIP
(see recipe page 26)

**QUESO
FONDUE-DO**
(see recipe page 27)

FRENCH ONION COB DIP Serves 12

almost
1
SERVE VEG
per serve

Here I've combined two of my all-time favourite dips: French onion, and spinach and artichoke — totally inspired by the classic old '70s and '80s cob dip, a ubiquitous staple at every Aussie barbecue and party. I've been there many a time. I'm completely guilty of throwing together a dip with a few tubs of sour cream, a packet of French onion soup mix and a box of chopped frozen spinach. And while I cringe at the very thought of it, I'd always be the one sitting within arm's length of the loaf to devour the lot. I wish I was exaggerating! Making the yoghurt-based Sour-ish cream on page 192 for this recipe is totally worth it, and offers a much healthier alternative to regular sour cream.

2 tablespoons extra virgin olive oil
   or butter (or a combination)
2 large onions, halved and thinly sliced
250 g (9 oz) bunch English spinach,
   with roots intact
2 garlic cloves, finely chopped
   or crushed
1 tablespoon thyme leaves
1 wholemeal cob loaf
⅔ cup (150 g) coarsely chopped
   marinated artichokes
1½–2 cups (400–550 g) Sour-ish cream
   (page 192)

Heat the oil in a large frying pan over medium heat. Sauté the onion for 15 minutes, stirring regularly. Season with sea salt and freshly ground black pepper.

Meanwhile, trim the roots from the spinach and wash the stems and leaves very well to remove any grit. Tie kitchen string around the stems and place the bunch in a large heatproof bowl, folding the leaves over if necessary. Pour over enough boiling water to cover. Leave for 1–2 minutes, or until wilted, then drain and cool under cold running water. Squeeze out as much excess water as possible, keeping the spinach in a log shape to make it easier to cut. Discard the string, then thinly slice the spinach and set aside.

After the onion has been cooking for 15 minutes, stir in the garlic and thyme and cook for a further 3 minutes, or until the onion and garlic are golden and caramelised. Set aside to cool completely.

Preheat the oven to 180°C (350°F). Using a serrated knife, cut a 2.5 cm (1 inch) thick slice from the top of the cob loaf, then tear or cut the bit you removed into bite-sized pieces. Leaving a 1 cm (½ inch) border of the crust intact, remove and tear the soft bread from the centre of the loaf into bite-sized pieces, creating a bread 'bowl'.

Place the bread 'bowl' and torn bread chunks on a large baking tray and bake for 5–10 minutes, or until golden and crisp.

Meanwhile, transfer the caramelised onion mixture to a food processor. Add the spinach, artichokes and 1½ cups (400 g) of the sour-ish cream and blend until the dip is your desired consistency, adding more sour-ish cream to taste. Season to taste with sea salt.

Spoon the dip into the bread bowl and serve immediately, with the toasted bread chunks as dippers.

TOP TIPS
- Add more sour-ish cream if you would prefer a dip that is less chunky.
- You may want to add 1 tablespoon lemon juice to cut through the richness of the dip.

(see photo page 24)

Almost 1½ serves wholegrains per serve

MAKE AHEAD
You can make the dip up to 5 days in advance. Store in an airtight container in the fridge.

VEGETARIAN • GLUTEN FREE • NUT FREE • EGG FREE

QUESO FONDUE-DO Serves 4–6

1/2 SERVE VEG per serve

What's not to love about the thought of hot melted cheese? Sadly, I find the idea of it is often better in theory, as feelings of regret too often set in when all that seemingly solidified cheese starts sitting heavy in the belly. Here's a much lighter version of Swiss fondue meets Mexican queso fundido, with a few other good-for-you ingredients thrown in — but taste wise, no one will know any different. Typically, queso fundido is served with crumbled chorizo on top, but lacto-vegetarians will love this version.

12 corn tortillas, each cut into 6 wedges
olive oil spray
3 cups (750 ml) White sauce (page 193)
½ cup (60 g) coarsely grated melty
   cheese, such as provolone or fontina
¼ cup (50 g) sun-dried or semi-dried
   tomatoes in oil, finely chopped,
   plus 2 tablespoons of the oil
½ teaspoon smoked paprika
1 spring onion (scallion), thinly sliced

Preheat the oven to 200°C (400°F). Line two large baking trays with baking paper.

Spread the tortilla wedges on the baking trays in a single layer. Spray both sides of the tortilla wedges with oil and lightly season with sea salt. Bake for 8–10 minutes, or until dry and golden, switching the trays around halfway through cooking.

Meanwhile, warm the white sauce and cheese in a saucepan over medium–low heat for 3–5 minutes, stirring often, until the mixture is hot and the cheese has melted. Keep warm over low heat.

Heat the sun-dried tomato oil in a small frying pan over medium–low heat. Add the tomatoes and paprika and cook for 2 minutes, or until fragrant, allowing the flavours to infuse.

Transfer the warm cheese mixture to a bowl and drizzle with the sun-dried tomato mixture. Scatter with the spring onion and serve immediately, with the tortilla wedges.

TOP TIP

• If you would like to serve this at a party, you can prepare everything you need beforehand, including the sun-dried tomato oil mixture. Melt the cheese and heat up the white sauce just before serving.

(see photo page 25)

VEGAN • DAIRY FREE • GLUTEN FREEABLE • EGG FREE

POPPIN' POTATO PANCAKES Makes 4

These tasty pancakes are inspired by Korean potato pancakes, which usually use potato starch, giving them a really nice chewy, gelatinous texture. If you're not so fond of the texture, you can use cornflour instead of potato starch, which is more widely available. I find equal parts of each is a happy medium.

1¹/2
SERVES VEG
per pancake

500 g (1 lb 2 oz) starchy/floury
    potatoes, peeled
1 small white or brown onion, peeled
¾ teaspoon fine sea salt
¼ teaspoon bicarbonate of soda
    (baking soda)
4 tablespoons potato starch
    or cornflour (or a combination)
neutral-flavoured oil, such as
    grapeseed or rice bran,
    for pan-frying

To serve
Bang bang sauce (page 194),
    for drizzling
kecap manis, for drizzling
Sesame salt (page 200), for sprinkling
coriander (cilantro) leaves, to garnish

Preheat the oven to 150°C (300°F).

Grate the potatoes and onion into a large bowl, being sure to leave any juices from the potatoes and onion in the bowl. (Alternatively, coarsely chop them, then process in a blender or food processor until very finely chopped, then transfer the chopped vegies and any liquid to a large bowl.)

Stir in the salt, bicarbonate of soda and potato starch until well combined.

Pour enough oil into a frying pan to lightly cover the base and place over medium heat until the oil is hot. Cooking the pancakes one at a time, add one-quarter of the mixture (about ⅔ cup) for each pancake, spreading it out with a back of a spoon to about 5 mm (¼ inch) thick. Cook for 3 minutes on each side, or until golden and cooked through.

Drain on paper towel and keep warm in the oven while cooking the remaining pancake batter.

Serve the pancakes warm, drizzled with the dressing and kecap manis, and sprinkled with sesame salt and coriander.

TOP TIPS
- If you leave the batter too long, a black layer will form on the surface due to oxidisation. It isn't at all harmful; you can simply scrape it off and use the batter without any concern.
- Kecap manis isn't essential — especially for those who can't eat gluten — but it does top these pancakes off. You can find it in Asian grocery stores and some supermarkets. (For gluten-free pancakes, use a gluten-free kecap manis, which is sometimes labelled 'sweet soy sauce'.)
- Potato starch is stocked by Asian grocers and many health food stores.

HEALTHY FATS
LOW CARB
LOW SATURATED FAT
NO CHOLESTEROL

VEGETARIAN • VEGAN-ABLE • DAIRY FREEABLE • NUT FREE

CORN DOGS TO BE PROUD OF Makes 8

Complete with the sauce — and you must make the sauce! — these beauties are a far cry from terrible fun-fair food, and the perfect party snack. Close your eyes and be transported to a fun park.

2
SERVES VEG
per corn dog

8 baby carrots, the size of small
   frankfurters
1 tablespoon olive oil
¼ teaspoon garlic powder (optional)
½ teaspoon smoked paprika (optional)
1 quantity (3 cups) Creamed corn
   (page 213)
1½ cups (225 g) plain flour
2¼ teaspoons baking powder
neutral-flavoured oil, for shallow-frying

Mustard mayo
3 tablespoons Mayo (page 192)
1 tablespoon American or German
   mustard
¼ teaspoon Tabasco sauce (optional)

Soak 8 thick bamboo skewers in water for at least 30 minutes.

Meanwhile, preheat the oven to 200°C (400°F).

Scrub or peel the carrots. In a shallow baking dish, combine the oil with the garlic powder and smoked paprika, if using. Season with sea salt and freshly ground black pepper, add the carrots and toss to coat. Roast for 25–30 minutes, or until tender when pierced with a skewer. Remove and set aside to cool.

Meanwhile, place the creamed corn, flour and baking powder in a bowl. Season with salt and pepper and mix to combine. Chill the mixture in the freezer for 20 minutes to firm up.

Combine the mustard mayo ingredients in a bowl and transfer to a squeezy bottle if you have one.

Insert a soaked skewer lengthways into each carrot, about two-thirds of the way through, starting from the thinner end or 'bottom' of the carrot.

Mould one-eighth (about ½ cup) of the chilled corn mixture around each carrot; don't worry too much if the coating isn't smooth. You can place the dogs in the freezer for about 10 minutes to firm up while you heat the oil, then smooth the coating out with your hand.

Reheat the oven to 150°C (300°F). Pour enough oil into a large frying pan to come 2.5 cm (1 inch) up the side. Heat the oil to 180°C (350°F), or until a cube of bread dropped into the oil turns golden brown in 15 seconds.

In several batches, cook the corn dogs for 4 minutes, or until golden, turning to colour all over. Drain well on paper towel and keep warm in the oven while cooking the remaining corn dogs.

Serve the corn dogs hot, with the mustard mayo.

TOP TIPS
- The smoked paprika and garlic powder give the carrots a 'meaty' flavour profile. If you don't have any, use a smoky barbecue spice blend instead.
- When inserting the skewers in the carrots, make sure your corn dogs will fit in your frying pan. You may need to trim your skewers slightly to accommodate them.
- To make the corn dogs vegan and dairy free, use olive oil instead of butter when making the Creamed corn.

HEALTHY FATS

Low cholesterol (2 mg per serve)

MAKE AHEAD
Make a double batch and freeze half the coated roasted carrots in an airtight container for up to 3 months. Allow the coating to thaw slightly (it should still be firm) before adding the corn dogs to the hot oil, as you want them to be hot in the centre.

VEGETARIAN • VEGAN-ABLE • DAIRY FREEABLE • NUT FREE • EGG FREE

WHEELY GOOD PIZZA SCROLLS Makes 12

Just as you can with pizza, you can mix and match your 'topping' ingredients here. There's a heap of flavour in the ones I've suggested, which get hidden in the rolled-up dough. If your family isn't overly fond of them, you can use the Pepperini on page 209 instead — but I'd still aim to get the artichokes in there, as they fly under the radar pretty easily. I like to add some coarsely chopped anchovies, too. These scrolls make a great lunchbox or afternoon tea snack.

almost
1
SERVE VEG
per scroll

1 quantity Pizza dough (page 205)
½ quantity Pizza sauce (page 206)
½ cup (100 g) coarsely chopped marinated artichokes
⅓ cup (60 g) pitted black or green olives (or a combination)
2 teaspoons baby capers in brine, drained
⅓ cup (50 g) grated provolone or buffalo mozzarella
chilli flakes, to taste (optional)

Preheat the oven to 200°C (350°F). Line a large baking tray with baking paper.

Place the dough on a lightly floured surface and roll out into a 35 × 25 cm (14 × 10 inch) rectangle, about 1 cm (½ inch) thick.

Spread the pizza sauce evenly over the top, leaving a 2 cm (¾ inch) border. Scatter all the topping ingredients over.

Carefully, and as tightly as possible, roll the dough up along the longest edge to make a log shape. Using a sharp knife, cut into 12 evenly sized pieces.

Lay the scrolls flat on the lined baking tray, about 2.5 cm (1 inch) apart. Cover with a tea towel and set aside in a warm place for 30 minutes, or until the scrolls have almost doubled in size.

Bake for 20–25 minutes, or until golden and cooked. Enjoy warm, or at room temperature.

TOP TIPS
- The dough is quite soft, so don't worry if you don't end up with the most perfectly shaped scrolls. I actually like them a bit wonky!
- To make the scrolls vegan and dairy free, omit the cheese.

LOW CARB
LOW CHOLESTEROL
LOW SATURATED FAT

- Almost 1 serve wholegrains per scroll
- ½ serve legumes per scroll

MAKE AHEAD
The scrolls will keep for up to 3 days in an airtight container in the fridge. Bring to room temperature before serving, or gently reheat in a hot oven.

THE NEW SAUSAGE ROLL Makes 12

It's hard to go past a freshly baked sausage roll, with its luscious layers of buttery crisp puff pastry. But here's a much healthier version you can indulge in more often — and even I was surprised at how tasty these are! A commercially made sausage roll typically has more than six times the saturated fat, double the calories, and more than double the carbohydrates as these ones... so tuck in.

almost
1
SERVE VEG
per serve

1 red onion, finely grated

2 garlic cloves, crushed or finely chopped

400 g (14 oz) tin butterbeans or borlotti beans, drained well

2 small or 1 large carrot, peeled and coarsely grated

2 small or 1 large zucchini (courgette), coarsely grated

2 tablespoons finely chopped sage

1½ teaspoons ground fennel or toasted fennel seeds

1 cup (105 g) instant oats

300 g (10½ oz) minced pork

1 egg, beaten, plus 1 egg yolk

1½ teaspoons fine sea salt

15 sheets filo pastry (from a 375 g/13 oz packet)

2 tablespoons extra virgin olive oil, plus extra for brushing

poppy seeds or Sesame salt (page 200), for sprinkling

Chunky tomato ketchup (page 226), to serve

Preheat the oven to 180°C (350°F). Line a large baking tray with baking paper.

Place the onion, garlic and butterbeans in a large bowl. Using a stick blender or masher, work the mixture into a coarse paste.

Using your hands, squeeze out and discard as much excess liquid as possible from the grated carrot and zucchini, then add them to the butterbean mixture with the sage, fennel, oats, pork, beaten egg and salt. Season with freshly ground black pepper and mix with your hands for about 1 minute, working the mixture until very well combined.

Remove the filo pastry from the packet and keep covered with a damp tea towel. Stack five sheets of pastry on top of each other on a clean work surface, spraying well or lightly brushing with oil in between each layer. Divide the filling mixture into thirds. Starting at the longest side closest to you, shape one portion of the filling along all the way out to the two shorter edges. Roll up to enclose the filling, then carefully cut into four sausage rolls. Repeat with the remaining pastry and filling.

In a small bowl, whisk the egg yolk with the 2 tablespoons oil. Lightly and evenly brush the mixture all over the sausage rolls. Lightly sprinkle poppy seeds or sesame salt along the centre of each.

Bake for 40 minutes, or until golden and cooked through. Enjoy warm, with ketchup.

TOP TIPS

- You can shape the filling into a meatloaf and bake it in a 4 cup (1 litre) loaf tin at 180°C (350°F), for about 40 minutes, until cooked through; I like to serve the meatloaf with a potato and parsnip mash.
- Instead of pork and sage in the filling or meatloaf, try beef and oregano, or lamb and rosemary.

LOW CARB
LOW SATURATED FAT

MAKE AHEAD
Filo pastry doesn't freeze well once cooked, but you can refrigerate the cooked rolls in an airtight container for 3 days; gently reheat in the oven. A raw batch of filling can be frozen for up to 3 months, well wrapped and protected from freezer burn.

CHANGE-YOUR-LIFE CHICKEN NUGGETS

Makes 20 | Serves 4–6

These little nuggets of goodness contain a little chicken liver, which is highly nutritious. They're also a brilliant way to sneak in some broccoli, which completely masks the liver flavour. A friend of mine once told me how she would buy a burger from a fast food restaurant, take it home, keep the best bits and then construct her own. You could certainly pull off a similar trick with these health-boosting nuggets, masquerading them as the 'real' deal, and diners would be none the wiser. Instead of deep-frying them, you could also bake them for about 10 minutes in a 190°C (375°F) oven, spraying them with oil beforehand. Turn the nuggets into a main meal by serving them with Creamed corn (page 213), Roasted potato mash (page 218), or blanched vegetables such as broccoli, peas and green beans.

almost
**1/2
SERVE VEG**
per
4 nuggets

1½–2 cups (90–120 g) fresh
   breadcrumbs, such as gluten-free
   or spelt
2½ cups (150 g) coarsely chopped
   broccoli
300 g (10½ oz) boneless, skinless
   chicken thighs or breast, trimmed
   of any excess fat, coarsely chopped
100 g (3½ oz) Chicken liver pâté
   (page 234)
neutral-flavoured oil, for shallow-frying
Chunky tomato ketchup (page 226),
   to serve (optional)

Preheat the oven to 120°C (235°F). Put the breadcrumbs in a shallow bowl.

Finely chop the broccoli using a food processor. Add the chicken and pâté, season well with sea salt and freshly ground black pepper and pulse to combine.

Form the mixture into nugget shapes, using 1 heaped tablespoon for each. Coat the nuggets well in the breadcrumbs.

Pour enough oil into a large frying pan to come up 1.5 cm (⅝ inch) up the side and place over medium heat. Heat the oil to 180°C (350°F), or until a cube of bread dropped into the oil turns golden brown in 15 seconds.

In batches, cook the nuggets for 2 minutes on each side, or until golden and cooked through. Drain well on paper towel and keep warm in the oven while cooking the remaining nuggets.

Serve warm, with chunky tomato ketchup if desired.

TOP TIPS
- If you don't want to use a food processor, you can cut or grate the broccoli, and use minced chicken.
- To make the nuggets gluten free, use gluten-free breadcrumbs.

LOW CARB

- Almost 1 serve protein in 4 nuggets
- 100% RDI vitamin B$_{12}$ in 4 nuggets

BATCH COOK
Make a double batch and freeze some crumbed, uncooked nuggets in an airtight container for up to 3 months. Layer them between sheets of baking paper before freezing, so they're touching as little as possible. Allow to thaw before cooking.

VEGETARIAN • DAIRY FREEABLE • GLUTEN FREEABLE

CHEESY CAULI POPCORN Serves 4–6

You'll find this is the easiest rendition of popcorn anything. And even better, you can whack it into the oven and not have to worry about any hot oil on the stove. These are best served fresh from the oven, though gobbling them up fast won't be a problem.

**1+
SERVES VEG
per serve**

1 cup (60 g) fresh breadcrumbs, such as gluten-free or spelt (see tips)

⅔ cup (60 g) finely grated parmesan cheese (see tips)

1 teaspoon ground turmeric

1 teaspoon garlic powder

½ cup (75 g) Sesame salt (page 200) or sesame seeds

2 eggs

4 cups (500 g) cauliflower, cut into 2 cm (¾ inch) pieces

extra virgin olive oil, for spraying or drizzling

Preheat the oven to 180°C (350°F). Line two baking trays with baking paper.

Put the breadcrumbs, parmesan, turmeric, garlic powder and sesame salt in a bowl. Season with sea salt and freshly ground black pepper and mix well to combine. In another shallow bowl, lightly beat the eggs.

Working with a few pieces at a time, dip the cauliflower florets in the beaten eggs, covering well, then in the breadcrumb mixture until well coated.

Spread the crumbed cauliflower in a single layer on the baking trays and spray or drizzle well with oil.

Bake for 20–25 minutes, or until golden, crisp and cooked through. Serve immediately.

TOP TIPS

- I like to make my own breadcrumbs whenever I see reduced-price spelt bread at my local organic supermarket — the older the better. I just whiz it up in a food processor and store the crumbs in biodegradable freezer bags in the freezer, where they'll keep for up to 6 months. If you're going to buy breadcrumbs, take a quick look at the ingredients and make sure the list isn't too long with 'stuff'.
- For dairy-free popcorn, replace the cheese with 1 tablespoon nutritional yeast flakes.
- To make the nuggets gluten free, use gluten-free breadcrumbs.

**HEALTHY FATS
LOW CARB**

- ½ serve protein per serve
+ 150% RDI vitamin C (from cauliflower)
- No added sugars

MAKE AHEAD

You can crumb up a batch ready for baking and keep it in an airtight container the fridge for up to 1 day, or in the freezer for up to 3 months.

BYE-NANA BREAD Makes 1 loaf | Serves 10

As the name suggests, we are saying bye-bye to your everyday slice of banana bread — the one with triple the carbs, one-quarter of the fibre and half the protein — and saying hello to this carrot cake hybrid, with half a serve of fruit *and* veg in every slice.

1/2 SERVE VEG per serve

2 overripe bananas, frozen whole, then thawed

7 fresh pitted dates, finely chopped

4 eggs

1 parsnip, peeled and coarsely grated; you'll need about 1 cup (150 g)

1 carrot, peeled and coarsely grated; you'll need about 1 cup (150 g)

4 tablespoons extra virgin olive oil or melted coconut oil

2 teaspoons natural vanilla extract (optional)

2 teaspoons ground cinnamon

a large pinch of sea salt

3 cups (300 g) almond meal

⅓ cup (40 g) coarsely chopped walnuts (optional)

2 teaspoons baking powder

Preheat the oven to 160°C (315°F). Line a 4 cup (1 litre) loaf tin with baking paper.

Peel the bananas and place in a large bowl. Add the dates and purée with a stick blender, or mash with a fork. (Alternatively, combine the bananas and dates using a food processor or blender.)

Whisk in the eggs, then stir in the remaining ingredients, ending with the almond meal, walnuts and baking powder. Pour the mixture into the loaf tin.

Bake on the middle shelf of the oven for 1 hour, or until the loaf is golden and a skewer inserted in the middle comes out clean. Remove from the oven and set aside to cool for 10 minutes.

Remove the loaf from the tin and wrap in plastic wrap or a tea towel to help keep it moist. Cut into slices to serve.

TOP TIP

• After an hour of cooking, the surface of the bread can turn from a beautiful golden colour to a darker one very quickly, so be sure to keep an eye on it.

HEALTHY FATS
LOW CARB

• 1½ serves protein + ½ serve fruit per serve
• Good source of monounsaturated fat, which helps lower risk of heart disease
• No added sugars

MAKE AHEAD
The bread will keep in an airtight container for up to 5 days. You can slice and freeze individual portions to snack on at any time, for up to 6 months. Thaw it in the fridge before serving.

APPLE AND BERRY BIRCHER MUFFINS

Makes 12 standard muffins

When I found out what was in regular muffins — a much enjoyed morning snack, especially by kids — I was blown away. Absolutely full of sugar and refined carbohydrates, there's nothing good about them at all. This is my nod to all those muffins out there, except that a standard blueberry muffin has nearly seven times the amount of added sugar, more than double the calories and cholesterol, and triple the carbs of these ones. Most of the energy in these muffins comes from healthy fats, keeping you fuller for longer, instead of setting you up for a sugar crash. And kids will love them, too.

¾ cup (75 g) rolled oats

2 tablespoons chia seeds

270 ml (9½ fl oz) coconut milk

2 eggs

3 tablespoons honey, preferably raw

1 small ripe banana, peeled and
  coarsely chopped

2 green apples, about 300 g (10½ oz)

½ cup (60 g) fresh or frozen
  raspberries or blueberries
  (or a combination)

3 tablespoons shredded coconut

1 teaspoon ground cinnamon

1 cup (150 g) spelt or wholemeal
  plain flour

2 teaspoons baking powder

a large pinch of sea salt

Combine the oats, chia seeds and coconut milk in a bowl and set aside for 30 minutes for the oats to soften.

Preheat the oven to 180°C (350°F). Grease a 12-hole standard muffin tin, then line each hole with a scrunched-up piece of baking paper.

In a bowl, whisk together the eggs and honey until combined, using a hand whisk. Add the banana and mash with a fork. Coarsely grate the unpeeled apples into the bowl, discarding the cores. Fold in the oat mixture, berries, shredded coconut and cinnamon to combine, then gently fold in the flour, baking powder and sea salt until just combined.

Evenly divide the mixture among the muffin holes.

Bake for 30 minutes, or until the muffin tops are lightly golden, and a skewer inserted into a muffin comes out almost clean.

Remove from the oven and set aside to cool for 10 minutes, before turning out of the tin to serve warm. Alternatively, you can let the muffins cool completely, then store in an airtight container.

TOP TIPS

- You don't need to buy special muffin cases when making muffins. I scrunch up small squares of baking paper.
- You can also use a giant six-hole Texas muffin tin for these muffins — just note that they'll take longer to cook, as there'll be double the amount of mixture in each muffin hole.

✛
Almost 1 wholegrain serve per muffin

MAKE AHEAD
You can keep the muffins in an airtight container in the fridge for up to 5 days, and gently warm them in a microwave for serving. Alternatively, they can be frozen for up to 3 months, in an airtight container, or individually wrapped; thaw in the fridge overnight.

CHAPTER TWO

KEEPING IT LIGHT

MAPLE 'BACON' PANCAKES Makes 12 | Serves 4

1/2 SERVE VEG per serve

Processed meats such as bacon are just not that good for our bodies, so I feel my daughter is better off without them in her diet, or at least only on the very odd occasion. So, this recipe is just a bit of fun, as strawberries are never actually a hard sell when it comes to pancakes — but when they are cut into 'lardons' they look like the real-bacon deal. My theory is: if you don't introduce something into a diet, then it can't be craved. But these pancakes will be.

1 cup (150 g) buckwheat flour, spelt or wholemeal plain flour (or a combination)
1 teaspoon ground cinnamon
1 teaspoon baking powder
a large pinch of sea salt
2 eggs
⅔ cup (170 ml) coconut milk
2 tablespoons maple syrup, plus extra to serve
2 cups (250 g) finely grated peeled pumpkin
grapeseed oil, rice bran oil or butter, for pan-frying
250 g (9 oz) strawberries, hulled, cut into small 'lardons'

Preheat the oven to 100°C (200°F). Combine the flour, cinnamon, baking powder and salt in a large bowl and make a well in the centre.

In another bowl or jug, whisk together the eggs, coconut milk and maple syrup. Stir in the pumpkin. Pour the mixture into the well in the dry ingredients and incorporate until just combined. Set aside to rest for 10 minutes, if using a gluten-based flour such as spelt or wholemeal.

Heat 1 tablespoon oil or butter in a large frying pan over medium heat. Working in batches, pour ¼ cup (60 ml) of the batter into the pan for each pancake and cook for 2 minutes on each side, or until golden and cooked; depending on the size of your pan, you should be able to cook three at a time. Keep warm in the oven while cooking the remaining batter.

Serve the pancakes warm, topped with the strawberry lardons and drizzled with extra maple syrup.

TOP TIP
• To make the pancakes gluten free, use buckwheat flour.

• Almost 1.5 serves wholegrains per serve
• Almost 25% RDI folate per serve

BATCH COOK
Make a double batch and store some in an airtight container in the fridge for up to 3 days, or in the freezer for up to 6 months. They make a great little snack on the go, and can even be reheated in the toaster if it has a crumpet (or similar) setting.

VEGAN-ABLE • DAIRY FREEABLE • GLUTEN FREE • NUT FREE • EGG FREE

NO-QUESO-DILLAS Serves 4

Minus the guacamole and herb garnish, these Mexican 'toasties' are perfect for the 'white food diet' that is often followed by fussy young children. The name of this dish is a bit subversive, because these are not your regular quesadillas. Sprinkling them with cheese is optional, but adds an appealing texture, like a parmesan crisp, so all the goodness inside will just get gobbled up.

**1
SERVE VEG
per serve**

12 corn tortillas
1½ cups (375 ml) White sauce
 (page 193), made with
 cannellini beans
3–4 tablespoons pickled jalapeño
 chillies, drained and chopped
 (optional)
olive oil, for drizzling or spraying,
 and pan-frying
⅔ cup (75 g) finely grated parmesan
 or pecorino cheese (optional)
1 ripe avocado
1 lime, cut in half
1 handful coriander (cilantro), sprigs
 picked, stems very finely chopped

Preheat the oven to 150°C (300°F).

Lay out six tortillas on a clean work surface. Spread about 3 tablespoons white sauce over each one and scatter with the jalapeño chilli, if using. Top with the remaining tortillas, lightly drizzle or spray with oil and sprinkle the tops with the cheese, if using.

Heat 2 teaspoons oil at a time in a frying pan over medium heat; to speed things up, you could use two frying pans, if you have them. Add a tortilla to the pan, cheese side down. Lightly drizzle with more oil and lightly season with sea salt. Cook for 2–3 minutes on each side, until golden. Transfer to the oven to keep warm while cooking the remaining tortillas, using more oil as needed.

Meanwhile, make some guacamole. Mash the avocado in a bowl. Juice half the lime and stir the juice through the avocado with the chopped coriander stems. Season to taste with salt and mix until well combined.

Cut the remaining lime into thin wedges. Cut the no-queso-dillas into wedges and serve warm, with the guacamole, coriander sprigs and lime wedges.

TOP TIP
• **For a vegan or dairy-free version, omit the cheese.**

**HEALTHY FATS
LOW CHOLESTEROL
(18 MG PER SERVE)**

• ½ serve dairy per serve
• Good source of monounsaturated fat
 (mostly from avocado and olive oil)
• No added sugars

VEGAN • DAIRY FREE • GLUTEN FREE • NUT FREE

PROPER BAKED BEANS Serves 4

Baked beans for breakfast when I was a kid, and even as a bigger kid, was something I'd get excited about. Sweet, saucy beans served on white toast slathered with margarine: so delicious, but hardly the most nutritious start to the day. I've tweaked the old classic into something you can feel good about dishing up to your family. This recipe is so easy to prepare that it seems criminal to revert to the tinned stuff. It also has fewer calories, half the carbs and is higher in healthy fats, which means you'll stay fuller for longer — a much better way to start the day.

2 × 400 g (14 oz) tins cannellini or borlotti beans (or a combination), drained well, reserving 3 tablespoons of the canning liquid (aquafaba; see tips)

1 roasted red capsicum (pepper), chopped (optional)

400 ml (14 fl oz) Roasted tomato passata (page 207), or store-bought tomato passata (puréed tomatoes)

2 teaspoons smoked paprika

a large pinch of cayenne pepper (optional)

2 teaspoons dijon mustard

1–2 tablespoons maple syrup, to taste

toasted gluten-free bread, to serve

chopped parsley, to garnish

Place the drained beans in a saucepan with the roasted capsicum, passata, spices, mustard and 1 tablespoon of the maple syrup. Stir until well combined, then bring to a simmer over medium heat. Cook for 10 minutes to allow the flavours to infuse, adding the reserved aquafaba for a thinner consistency, if desired.

Season well with sea salt and freshly ground black pepper, adding more maple syrup for extra sweetness if desired.

Serve hot, with toasted crusty bread, garnished with chopped parsley.

TOP TIPS

- Aquafaba ('bean water') can be used in this recipe, as well as the Tropical pavlova on page 185 and the Mayo on page 192. In this recipe, it's useful as it is thicker than water, and won't thin out the sauce as much as water would. Aquafaba is often used in vegan cooking as an egg replacement.
- Start with a lesser amount of maple syrup to begin with and add to taste; tinned baked beans are quite sweet.
- Homemade passata is great in this recipe, adding a natural sweetness.
- The paprika and cayenne pepper add a lovely smokiness, so bacon lovers will hardly miss their bacon.

**HEALTHY FATS
NO CHOLESTEROL
LOW SATURATED FAT**

- 1 serve legumes + almost 1 serve protein per serve
- 270% RDI vitamin C + 65% RDI folate per serve
- Great source of fibre

MAKE AHEAD
The cooked beans will keep in an airtight container in the fridge for up to 3 days.

ASIAN-STYLE COLESLAW Serves 4

Coleslaw is one of those all-time favourite salads, usually doused in loads of mayo, but I love this mayo-free coleslaw with its Asian-style flavours, which really lighten it up, while delivering heaps of flavour. The bed of smashed avocado on the serving plate really brings it all together. This salad always seems to go down well when taken to a party, or whenever friends come over. Adding some prawns or smoked fish is a great option when you're feeling a bit fancy. Shredded poached chicken works well, too.

2 SERVES VEG per serve

¼ Chinese cabbage, thinly sliced

1 carrot, peeled, then shredded or grated

1 baby fennel bulb, very thinly sliced

2 celery stalks, very thinly sliced diagonally

100 g (3½ oz) snow peas (mangetout), thinly sliced diagonally

2 spring onions (scallions), very thinly sliced

4 tablespoons fish sauce or gluten-free soy sauce

4 tablespoons rice vinegar, plus extra for drizzling

1½ tablespoons sesame oil

1½ tablespoons maple syrup, or 1 tablespoon raw or white sugar

2 ripe avocados, peeled

1 tablespoon lime juice

a pinch of sea salt

100 g (3½ oz) hot smoked trout or salmon, or halved cooked prawns (optional)

Combine the cabbage, carrot, fennel, celery, snow peas and spring onion in a large bowl.

In another bowl, whisk together the fish sauce, vinegar, sesame oil and maple syrup until well combined. Drizzle the dressing over the vegetables and toss well to combine.

Mash the avocados in a bowl with the lime juice and salt. Spread the mashed avocado over a serving platter and top with the coleslaw. Flake the fish over the top, if using, and serve immediately.

DIVIDE AND CONQUER

- Serving the prawns or smoked fish on the side is an easy option for those who would like fish.
- To make the coleslaw vegan, use soy sauce rather than fish sauce, and omit the seafood.
- Make half the dressing vegan by dividing the vinegar, sesame oil and maple syrup between two small bowls, then add half the fish sauce to one bowl, and half the soy sauce to the other bowl.

**HEALTHY FATS
LOW CARB**

✚

- Over 50% RDI vitamin A per serve

MAKE AHEAD

You can prepare the coleslaw ahead, keeping the salad and dressing separate. To stop the fennel discolouring, soak the slices in water with a dash of vinegar. Drain well and toss through the salad just before serving.

TOP COBB SALAD Serves 4–6

Candied smoky walnuts step in as an admirable replacement for the bacon element in this salad. They're such tasty little treasures that down to the very last mouthful, you'll be asking, 'What bacon — who needs bacon?' For extra texture and a bit of bite, add some thinly sliced radishes to the salad.

1 SERVE VEG per serve

2 tablespoons red wine vinegar

3 tablespoons extra virgin olive oil

1 teaspoon dijon or wholegrain mustard

1 cos or iceberg lettuce, coarsely chopped

250 g (9 oz) grape or cherry tomatoes, halved

1 Lebanese cucumber, coarsely chopped

1 ripe avocado, coarsely chopped

250 g (9 oz) shredded poached chicken from the Chicken stock on page 220, or barbecued chicken (optional)

2 hard-boiled eggs (see tip), shelled and grated

Candied walnuts

1½ tablespoons maple syrup

½ teaspoon smoked paprika

scant ½ teaspoon fine sea salt

½ cup (50 g) walnuts

To make the candied walnuts, combine the maple syrup, paprika and salt in a small saucepan over low heat. Stir in the walnuts and cook for 4 minutes, or until the maple syrup completely dries out and coats the walnuts. Spread the candied walnuts in a single layer on a tray lined with baking paper and allow to cool completely.

In a large serving bowl, whisk together the vinegar, oil and mustard. Season with sea salt and freshly ground black pepper, add the lettuce, tomatoes and cucumber and toss to combine.

Scatter the avocado over the top, along with the chicken, if using. Scatter the grated egg over, top with the walnuts and serve immediately.

TOP TIP

- To boil eggs, bring them to room temperature (so the shells don't crack), place them in a saucepan, cover with plenty of cold water and slowly bring to a gentle boil. For **SOFT-BOILED EGGS**, cook at a gentle simmer for 4 minutes. For **MEDIUM-BOILED EGGS**, simmer for 5 minutes. For **HARD-BOILED EGGS**, simmer for 8 minutes. Remove the eggs with a slotted spoon and plunge into cold water to stop them cooking further. Some people like to add a splash of vinegar to the cooking water, to set the egg whites if the shells happen to crack.

DIVIDE AND CONQUER

- For a vegan salad, omit the eggs and chicken.
- To cater for vegetarians, serve the chicken separately, and adjust the quantity of chicken accordingly.

**HEALTHY FATS
LOW CARB**

- ½ serve protein per serve (without chicken)
- 1½ serves protein per serve (with chicken)
- Good source of monounsaturated fat

MAKE AHEAD

The candied walnuts will keep for up to 2 days in an airtight container at room temperature. They also make a great snack!

CORN AND CHICKEN SOUP Serves 4

Chicken and corn soup (and crabmeat and corn soup) from the local Chinese restaurant was a childhood staple in our household, and is filled with fond memories for me. This popular crowd pleaser also provides the perfect opportunity to sneak in other hidden treasures and bump up that veg count. If you're short of time, instead of poaching the chicken in the stock, you can divide a shredded barbecued chicken breast among individual bowls — or, to make the soup a little special, use some picked crabmeat, which you can buy in small tubs from fishmongers and selected supermarkets.

2¹/₂ SERVES VEG per serve

2 teaspoons sesame oil, plus extra
    for drizzling
4 spring onions (scallions), quartered
    lengthways, then thinly sliced
8 cups (2 litres) Chicken stock
    (page 220)
115 g (4 oz) punnet of fresh baby corn
    (see tips), coarsely chopped, or a
    425 g (15 oz) tin baby corn, drained
    and chopped (see tips)
1 chicken breast, weighing 180–250 g
    (6–9 oz)
1 tablespoon cornflour
3 tablespoons light soy sauce
1 tablespoon finely grated fresh ginger
½ quantity (1½ cups) Creamed corn
    (page 213)
1 large corn cob, kernels removed, or
    1⅓ cups (200 g) frozen corn kernels
2 eggs, lightly beaten
225 g (8 oz) tin bamboo strips, drained
    (see tips)

To serve
spring onions (scallions), thinly sliced
    on an angle
coriander (cilantro) sprigs
freshly ground white pepper (see tips)

Heat the sesame oil in a large saucepan over medium heat. Cook the spring onion for 2 minutes, or until softened. Pour in the stock. If using fresh baby corn, add it now and bring the stock to a simmer.

Add the whole chicken breast, then reduce the heat to low and cover with a lid. Set a timer to 12 minutes for a 180 g (9 oz) breast, or 15 minutes for a 250 g (9 oz) breast. (If the stock starts to simmer, remove the lid to let some heat escape — you don't want the stock to simmer, or you'll overcook the chicken.)

Remove the poached chicken from the broth and set aside to rest. When cool enough to handle, shred the chicken and set aside.

In a bowl, mix the cornflour with a little of the broth to make a smooth slurry.

Add the soy sauce, ginger, creamed corn and corn kernels to the soup. (If using tinned baby corn, add it now.) Slowly stir in the cornflour slurry until combined. Slowly pour in the beaten eggs, waiting until they're completely poured in, then very gently stir.

Return the chicken to the pan with the bamboo shoots and warm for 1 minute. Season to taste with sea salt.

Serve the soup immediately, drizzled with a little more sesame oil, and sprinkled with the spring onion, coriander and white pepper, if using.

TOP TIPS

- To make the soup vegan and dairy free, use Mushroom stock (page 216) as the soup base, omit the chicken or crabmeat, and use olive oil instead of butter when making the creamed corn.
- For a gluten-free soup, use gluten-free soy sauce.
- After draining tinned corn or tinned bamboo shoots, I steep them in boiling water for 5 minutes to remove the overpowering brine flavour.
- I keep white peppercorns in my grinder — I absolutely love them! Freshly ground white pepper is fabulous with this soup, so do give it a go.

**HEALTHY FATS
HIGH IN PROTEIN
LOW CARB**

- Almost 1 serve protein per serve
- Almost 100% RDI vitamin B_3 per serve
- Chicken stock is a good source of vitamin B_{12}

MAKE AHEAD
Make a double batch, up until the point of adding the eggs, and store in an airtight container in the fridge for up to 3 days, or freeze for up to 3 months. To serve, gently reheat, then resume the recipe.

WHIZ-BANG FALAFEL Makes 16 | Serves 4

2 SERVES VEG per serve

Here is my cheat's homemade falafel, which fast-tracks the longer process of soaking dried chickpeas overnight. While the deep-fried version of *anything* nearly always wins for flavour, these baked goods are just as tasty and much easier to cook, without the mess of deep-frying. Chickpeas are a good source of iron and protein, so you won't be missing the meat, especially as they are seasoned with baharat, a Middle Eastern spice mix that imparts so much flavour. Thanks to the vitamin C in the dressing, the iron in the chickpeas is more easily absorbed by your body, too.

2 × 400 g (14 oz) tins chickpeas

2 cups coriander (cilantro) or parsley leaves and stems (or a combination)

2 French shallots or 1 small red onion, peeled and coarsely chopped

3 garlic cloves, peeled

1 egg white

2 teaspoons baking powder

⅓ cup (50 g) sesame seeds

2 teaspoons baharat or za'atar (or 1 teaspoon each ground coriander and cumin)

½ teaspoon fine sea salt

1 tablespoon extra virgin olive oil, plus extra for drizzling

Lemon tahini dressing

2 tablespoons lemon juice

4 tablespoons tahini

1½ tablespoons extra virgin olive oil

To serve

gluten-free flatbreads

salad and/or tabouleh

Drain the chickpeas well, but don't rinse them. Spread them in a single layer on a baking tray lined with baking paper. Thoroughly pat dry with paper towel, then place in the oven and turn the oven temperature to 220°C (425°F). As soon the oven comes to up to temperature, remove the tray from the oven and set aside, to slightly dry out the chickpeas while you prepare the remaining ingredients; leave the oven on.

Put the herbs, shallot and garlic in a food processor or blender. Reserving the baking paper and baking tray, add the chickpeas and blend until almost smooth. Add the remaining falafel ingredients and pulse to combine.

Shape the mixture into 16 evenly sized falafel balls and place on the lined baking tray. Drizzle them on both sides with a little extra oil and bake for 15 minutes, or until golden.

Meanwhile, whisk or blend the lemon tahini dressing ingredients with 4 tablespoons water until smooth. Season to taste with sea salt and set aside.

Serve the falafel warm, with flatbreads, salad or tabouleh, and the lemon tahini dressing.

TOP TIPS

- To keep the carbs low, ditch the flatbreads and serve the falafel with plenty of salad and tabouleh.
- Drying the chickpeas in the oven while it is preheating is the perfect way to dry them out just a little, to ensure they're not too mushy or sloppy.

HEALTHY FATS HIGH IN PROTEIN NO CHOLESTEROL

- 2 serves wholegrains + 50% RDI fibre per serve
- Almost 2 serves protein + almost 1½ serves legumes per serve
- Good source of iron (almost 30% RDI for women; over 60% for men and kids under 9)
- Good source of antioxidants, vitamin C and E

BATCH COOK

Make a double batch of falafel, shape into balls and freeze some in an airtight container between sheets of baking paper for up to 6 months; thaw in the fridge overnight before using. Alternatively, you can freeze the entire falafel mixture and shape it into balls once thawed.

FEEL GOOD FISH CAKES Makes 8 | Serves 4

There are lots of hidden treasures in these fish cakes. You'll have no trouble convincing the kids to try them! When Jerusalem artichokes are in season, definitely give them a go here. With their crisp outer layer and soft, potato mash–like centre, they're a delicious way to add some healthy variety to your family's diet.

**3¹/₂
SERVES VEG
per serve**

250 g (9 oz) scrubbed potatoes,
  with skins on
250 g (9 oz) scrubbed Jerusalem
  artichokes or sweet potatoes,
  with skins on
grapeseed or rice bran oil, for drizzling
  and shallow-frying
2 × 150 g (5½ oz) skinless, boneless
  salmon fillets (see tip)
400 g (14 oz) tin cannellini beans,
  drained well
2–3 spring onions (scallions), finely
  chopped
1 tablespoon finely chopped tarragon
  or dill
3 tablespoons finely chopped parsley
2 teaspoons capers, rinsed
1 egg, lightly beaten
1 lemon, zest finely grated, then
  cut into wedges
1 tablespoon plain flour
baby cos or mixed salad leaves,
  to serve
Mayo (page 192), to serve (optional)

For crumbing
2 eggs
2–3 cups (120–180 g) fresh
  breadcrumbs
plain flour, for dusting

Preheat the oven to 200°C (400°F). Cut the potatoes and Jerusalem artichokes into 1.5–2 cm (¾ inch) chunks. Place in a large baking dish, drizzle with oil and season with sea salt. Toss until combined, then roast for 15 minutes.

Add the salmon fillets to the baking dish and bake for a further 5 minutes, then remove from the oven. Set aside until cool enough to handle.

In a large bowl, lightly mash the roasted vegetables and cannellini beans. Add the spring onion, herbs, capers, egg, lemon zest and flour. Flake the salmon over, season with salt and freshly ground black pepper and mix until just combined.

Divide the mixture into eight portions and shape into patties. Chill the patties in the refrigerator for about 30 minutes to firm up.

Reheat the oven to 120°C (235°F). Set up a crumbing station: beat the eggs in a wide shallow bowl, and place the breadcrumbs and flour in separate bowls.

Pour enough oil into a large frying pan to come 1.5 cm (⅝ inch) up the side. Heat the oil to 180°C (350°F), or until a cube of bread dropped into the oil turns golden brown in 15 seconds.

Dust each fish patty in flour, shaking off any excess. Dip into the egg until well coated, then coat well in the breadcrumbs. Working in batches, fry the fish cakes for 3 minutes on each side, or until golden. Keep warm in the oven while cooking the remaining fish cakes.

Serve hot, with lemon wedges, salad leaves and mayo, if desired.

TOP TIPS

- **The fish cakes taste better fried, but you can also bake them in a preheated 220°C (425°F) oven for 15 minutes, until golden.**
- **It's often cheaper to buy salmon with the skin on. It slips off easily once baked. (I like to grill the skin into crispy 'chips' — my daughter loves them.)**
- **If you have a gluten allergy, use gluten-free flour and breadcrumbs.**

DIVIDE AND CONQUER

- **To make half the cakes vegetarian, use 2 × 400 g (14 oz) tins of beans and 1 salmon fillet. Mash one tin of beans with the patty ingredients and divide between two bowls. Add the salmon to one and the extra beans to the other.**

**HEALTHY FATS
HIGH IN PROTEIN**

- 1¼ serves legumes + 2 serves protein per serve
- 80% RDI vitamin B₁₂ per serve
- Great source of vitamin C
- No added sugars

MAKE AHEAD
Using fresh fish, shape and crumb the patties, but don't cook them. Place between sheets of baking paper, ensuring they don't touch each other, and freeze in an airtight container for up to 3 months. Thaw in the fridge overnight before cooking.

THAI BEET SALAD Serves 4

Lots of people love a Thai beef salad, but throw in some beets as an alternative option and suddenly vegetarians can get in on the action. This recipe is a fun and colourful way to keep both meat eaters and vegans happy, so everybody wins.

**3
SERVES VEG
per serve**

1 red Asian shallot or ½ small red onion, halved and very thinly sliced

½ quantity Tangy Asian dressing (page 195)

200 g (7 oz) rump steak

olive oil, for drizzling

150 g (5½ oz) snow peas (mangetout), trimmed

250 g (9 oz) cherry or grape tomatoes, halved

1 large Lebanese cucumber, coarsely chopped

4 radishes, very thinly sliced

1 carrot, scrubbed or peeled, then very thinly sliced

250 g (9 oz) cooked baby beetroot (see tips), drained and patted dry, thinly sliced

1 large handful of herbs, such as Thai basil, coriander (cilantro) and/or mint leaves

¼ cup (40 g) roasted unsalted peanuts, coarsely chopped

Combine the shallot and dressing in a large bowl; set aside until needed.

Drizzle the steak on both sides with oil and season with sea salt and freshly ground black pepper. Heat an unoiled frying pan over high heat. Once the pan is smoking, cook the beef for 1–2 minutes on each side for rare (depending on the thickness of the steak). Remove from the pan and set aside for 5 minutes to rest.

Meanwhile, bring a saucepan of salted water to the boil. Add the snow peas and cook for 2 minutes, or until tender. Drain and refresh under cold running water.

Very thinly slice the beef. Arrange all the ingredients on a large platter, drizzling with the shallot dressing and scattering with the herbs and peanuts. Serve immediately.

TOP TIPS

- Bring the steak out of the fridge and allow to come to room temperature before cooking.
- For a more substantial meal, cook 1 cup (200 g) long-grain brown rice to serve with it.
- You can buy great-quality precooked beetroot nowadays without anything added other than water. Always check the ingredients panel before buying any packaged goods.

DIVIDE AND CONQUER

- To make half the dish vegan, simply serve the beef to one side, and use soy sauce rather than fish sauce in the Tangy Asian dressing — or divide the palm sugar and lime juice between two small bowls, and add only half the soy sauce to one bowl, and only half the fish sauce to the other and serve the dressings on the side.

**LOW CARB
LOW SATURATED FAT**

- Almost 1 serve protein per serve (if using beef)
- Over 25% RDI fibre per serve
- High in vitamin C

WARM SALMON NIÇOISE Serves 4

Turning on the oven to prepare a salad may not seem very logical, but I find it's much easier to add a range of ingredients to a single baking tray rather than blanching them separately in pots of boiling water and fiddling about with colanders and the like. More importantly, it also means that valuable nutrients aren't leaching into the water, as they do when you boil vegetables. Of course, if you would prefer not to turn on the oven, you can easily steam the vegetables, which would be preferable to boiling them.

**3¹/₂
SERVES VEG
per serve**

750 g (1 lb 10 oz) kipfler (fingerling)
  or new potatoes, scrubbed, then
  cut into bite-sized chunks
olive oil, for drizzling
400 g (14 oz) skinless, boneless salmon
  or trout
250 g (9 oz) green beans, topped
  and halved
6–8 asparagus spears, trimmed,
  halved crossways
½ cup (100 g) marinated artichokes,
  cut into small wedges
½ cup (75 g) pitted green olives
250 g (9 oz) grape or cherry tomatoes,
  halved
2 medium-boiled eggs (see tip on
  page 54), shelled and quartered

Herb and mustard dressing
4 tablespoons extra virgin olive oil,
  plus extra for drizzling
2 anchovies, very finely chopped
2 tablespoons lemon juice
2 teaspoons dijon mustard
1 tablespoon finely chopped tarragon,
  dill or parsley

Preheat the oven to 220°C (425°F) fan-forced. Line a large baking tray with baking paper.

Arrange the potatoes in a single layer on one side of the baking tray. Drizzle with oil, season with sea salt and freshly ground black pepper and toss to coat. Cover with foil and bake for 15 minutes.

Meanwhile, make the dressing. In a large bowl, whisk together the oil, anchovies, lemon juice and mustard until combined. Season to taste with salt and pepper, then stir in the tarragon.

After the potatoes have been baking for 15 minutes, add the salmon to the other side of the baking tray, along with the beans and asparagus. Drizzle with oil and season with salt and pepper. Return to the oven and bake for 5 minutes, or until the salmon is just cooked and the vegetables are just tender. Set aside for 5 minutes to cool slightly.

Add the beans, asparagus and potatoes to the bowl of dressing, along with the artichokes, olives and tomatoes. Toss to combine, then divide among serving bowls.

Flake the salmon over the top, garnish with the egg quarters and serve immediately.

TOP TIP
• **For an egg-free salad, leave out the boiled eggs.**

**HEALTHY FATS
LOW CARB**

• 1 serve protein per serve
• 100% RDI phosphorus + 35% RDI fibre per serve
• Good source of monounsaturated fat
(from salmon, extra virgin olive oil and olives)

VEGAN-ABLE • DAIRY FREEABLE • NUT FREEABLE • EGG FREE

FAUX CHEESE RAVIOLI Serves 4

Another twist on a familiar classic, here's my version of a four-cheese ravioli
— one which is a good source of healthy fats and actually contains very little
cheese! You don't even have to use the cheese, though it's only a small quantity,
and more about tricking the kids as to how much (or rather, how little) melty
cheese is hidden inside these creamy-textured ravioli pillows. To the kids,
it's only the pronunciation that separates *four* from *faux*.

1½
SERVES VEG
per serve

30 round dumpling (gow gee) wrappers
1 cup (250 ml) White sauce (page 193)
⅓ cup (35 g) finely grated melty
    cheese, such as havarti or fontina
2 tablespoons extra virgin olive oil,
    plus extra for drizzling
1 handful of sage leaves
2 tablespoons pine nuts, toasted
700 ml (24 fl oz) Roasted tomato
    passata (page 207), or store-bought
    tomato passata (puréed tomatoes)

Bring a large saucepan of salted water to a simmer.

Meanwhile, half-fill a small bowl with water. Working in batches, lay out up
to five dumpling wrappers on a clean work surface. Put 3 teaspoons white sauce
into the centre of each and top with 1 teaspoon cheese. Lightly brush water
around the filling, then place another dumpling wrapper on top. Press the edges
together to enclose the filling, pushing out any air bubbles, and pressing firmly
around the edges of the wrappers to seal each ravioli.

Heat the oil in a large deep frying pan over medium–low heat. Add the sage
and pine nuts and cook for 2 minutes, or until the sage leaves turn crisp, dark
green and slightly translucent. Transfer the leaves, nuts and any oil to a small
bowl. Add the passata to the pan and cook for 5 minutes, stirring occasionally,
until heated through. Keep warm over low heat.

Working in batches, add the ravioli to the pan of simmering water and cook
for 3 minutes, or until they rise to the surface, gently stirring the pan to release
the ravioli from the bottom. Remove with a slotted spoon and transfer to a tray,
drizzling with extra oil to stop them sticking to one another. Keep warm.

Serve the ravioli immediately, drizzled with the passata and scattered with
the pine nuts, crispy sage leaves and any remaining oil, or a little extra oil.

TOP TIPS
• For a vegan or dairy-free dish, omit the cheese.
• For a nut-free dish, leave out the pine nuts.

HEALTHY FATS
LOW CARB

• ½ serve protein per serve
• Great source of dietary fibre
• Sage is a good (and main) source of calcium
• Good source of iron + great source of vitamin C,
    for better iron absorption

NICE FRIED RICE Serves 4

I'm not sure there are many people in the world who don't like fried rice. This one isn't your standard fried rice, as it uses brown basmati rice, which may seem a little strange — but I think its texture is as close as you can get to a fluffy long-grain white rice, while being far more nutritious. One thing is for certain: this fried rice will not disappoint.

1¹/₂ SERVES VEG per serve

¼ cup (50 g) quinoa (see tips)

200 g (1 cup) brown basmati rice (see tips)

2 eggs

1½ tablespoons dark soy sauce (or regular soy sauce)

2 tablespoons grapeseed, rice bran or coconut oil

1 tablespoon finely grated fresh ginger

2 garlic cloves, crushed or finely chopped

1 handful of garlic chives or coriander (cilantro), or a combination, cut into 3 cm (1¼ inch) lengths

3 cups (350 g) finely chopped cauliflower (see tips)

2 tablespoons sesame oil

4 tablespoons oyster sauce

4 large raw prawns, peeled and deveined, then cut into 1 cm (½ inch) pieces

100 g (3½ oz) fresh baby corn, rinsed and coarsely chopped, or ⅔ cup (100 g) frozen peas

100 g (3½ oz) punnet of snow pea sprouts, cut into thirds, or 1 cup (100 g) bean sprouts

Soak the quinoa in a bowl of water while bringing a saucepan of water to the boil.

Drain the quinoa through a very fine sieve, then add it to the pan of boiling water with the rice. Cook for 15 minutes, or until the rice is just tender.

Drain, then rinse in cold water to stop the grains cooking any further. Transfer to a shallow dish to cool and dry completely; you can even leave it overnight.

Crack the eggs into a bowl, add 1 teaspoon of the soy sauce and lightly whisk using a fork. Season with ground white pepper, or freshly ground black pepper.

Heat the oil in a wok or large deep frying pan over high heat. Add the beaten eggs and stir-fry for 20 seconds. Now add the ginger, garlic and any coriander stems, if using, and stir-fry for a further 20 seconds.

Add the rice mixture and cauliflower and drizzle with the sesame oil. Stir-fry for 3 minutes, then add the oyster sauce, remaining soy sauce and the prawns and stir-fry for 1 minute.

Add the corn, sprouts and any remaining herbs and stir-fry for a final 1–2 minutes, or until the sprouts have just wilted. Serve immediately.

TOP TIPS

- Giving the quinoa a good rinse or soak will remove the bitter saponin that coats the grains.
- If using white basmati rice, it won't take as long to cook as brown basmati, so boil the quinoa for 5 minutes before adding the rice, then cook the rice for 10 minutes, giving the quinoa a total cooking time of 15 minutes.
- If using a food processor to chop up the cauliflower, be careful not to take it too far, as the water that will come out of the cauliflower will make your rice lumpy and soft. To avoid this, chop the cauliflower by hand, or grate it.
- For a gluten-free dish, use gluten-free soy sauce and oyster sauce.

DIVIDE AND CONQUER

- To cater for vegans, use vegetarian oyster sauce, and replace the prawns and eggs with finely chopped mushrooms or chopped firm tofu.
- You can fry the prawns and eggs separately and scatter them over the non-vegan serves.

HEALTHY FATS

- 3½ serves wholegrains + ½ serve protein per serve
- Over 20% RDI iron (in the oyster sauce, quinoa and basmati rice) per serve
- Great source of vitamin C, for iron absorption

MAKE AHEAD

You can cook the rice and quinoa a day ahead and leave to dry out in the fridge overnight, then resume the recipe the next day.

VEGAN-ABLE • DAIRY FREEABLE • GLUTEN FREE • NUT FREEABLE • EGG FREE

MIX-IT-UP MINESTRONE Serves 4

I call this soup the 'hero' of all soups as it's such a great way to use up all those leftover vegetables, without having to think too hard about what to do with them all. It's also highly nutritious, with plenty of vitamins and minerals, and is easy on your digestive system, too. The vegetables I've used here are really just a guide, so feel free to use whatever you have on hand — I've even used Chinese broccoli! If using store-bought tomato passata, add a finely chopped onion and some garlic when sautéing the celery and carrot.

5
SERVES VEG
per serve

1 tablespoon extra virgin olive oil,
   plus extra to serve
1–2 celery stalks, coarsely chopped
1–2 carrots, scrubbed or peeled,
   quartered lengthways, then sliced
1 tablespoon thyme leaves, or any other
   favourite herb
4 cups (1 litre) Chicken stock (page 220)
   or Mushroom stock (page 216)
2 bay leaves (optional)
½ cup (100 g) dried soup mix, or a 400 g
   (14 oz) tin beans, such as borlotti
   beans, drained
300 g (10½ oz) potatoes or sweet
   potatoes, peeled or scrubbed,
   cut into 1.5 cm (⅝ inch) pieces
700 ml (24 fl oz) Roasted tomato
   passata (page 207), or store-bought
   tomato passata (puréed tomatoes)
100 g (3½ oz) green beans, trimmed
   and cut into thirds
1 zucchini (courgette), coarsely chopped
⅔ cup (100 g) frozen peas
200 g (7 oz) leafy greens, coarsely
   chopped, such as rainbow chard
   or spinach
⅓ cup (30 g) finely grated parmesan
   cheese, or grated macadamia nuts

Heat the oil in a large saucepan over medium heat. Add the celery, carrot and thyme and cook, stirring, for 3 minutes. Add the stock and bay leaves, if using.

If using the dried soup mix, stir it in now with an additional 2–3 cups (500–750 ml) water, bring to a simmer and cook for 15–20 minutes, or until the dried pulses are par-cooked. (If you are using tinned beans, omit this step.)

If using potato, add it to the soup and cook for 5 minutes; if using sweet potato, add it to the soup and cook for only 3 minutes.

Stir in the passata and return to a simmer, then add the green beans and cook for 5 minutes.

Add the zucchini, frozen peas and leafy greens, along with the tinned beans, if using. Cook for a further 5 minutes, or until all the ingredients are tender. Season to taste with sea salt and freshly ground black pepper.

Serve the soup drizzled with a little olive oil, and sprinkled with the grated parmesan or macadamias.

TOP TIPS
• If you have a parmesan rind in the fridge, add it to the pan when you're adding the stock, to impart more flavour.
• For a vegan soup, use mushroom stock as the soup base, and serve with macadamia nuts instead of cheese.
• For a dairy-free soup, serve with macadamia nuts instead of parmesan.
• For a nut-free soup, serve with parmesan instead of macadamias.

HEALTHY FATS
LOW CHOLESTEROL
(12 MG PER SERVE)

• ½ serve legumes per serve
• Great source of fibre + vitamin C
• Good source of magnesium

MAKE AHEAD
The soup will keep in an airtight container in the fridge for up to 3 days, or in the freezer for up to 6 months.

SHOUT LOUDER FOR THIS CHOWDER Serves 4

Take this classic to a whole new level by ditching the cream and using the creaminess and colour of a heap of puréed vegetables to add a velvety silkiness to the soup — along with loads of extra nutrients. No one will even know! There's stacks of flavour in prawn heads and shells, so making a stock from them, as we do below, is a great way to get the most from them. If you have an allergy or would prefer not to use them, use 4 cups (1 litre) fish or vegetable stock, and add a pinch of cayenne pepper if you like.

4 SERVES VEG per serve

2½ tablespoons butter

1 leek, white part only, halved lengthways, then thinly sliced

1 baby fennel bulb, cut into 1 cm (½ inch) pieces

2 garlic cloves, crushed or finely chopped

1 tablespoon extra virgin olive oil, plus extra for drizzling

½ teaspoon smoked paprika, plus extra to serve

250 g (9 oz) whole raw prawns, peeled and deveined, reserving the heads and shells, then cut in half lengthways

4 cups (500 g) cauliflower, cut into 2 cm (¾ inch) pieces

250 g (9 oz) potato, peeled and cut into 2 cm (¾ inch) pieces

1–2 corn cobs, kernels removed

150 g (5½ oz) boneless, skinless firm white fish, cut into 2 cm (¾ inch) pieces

100 g (3½ oz) boneless, skinless hot smoked salmon fillet, flaked into large pieces

4 tablespoons coarsely chopped parsley

In a large saucepan, melt half the butter over medium heat. Add the leek, fennel and garlic and cook for 3–5 minutes, or until softened, stirring often. Remove the mixture from the pan and set aside.

Increase the heat to medium–high and add the oil to the pan, along with the paprika and reserved prawn heads and shells. Cook for 1 minute, stirring constantly, until the prawn shells are bright red. Add 8 cups (2 litres) water, season well with sea salt and freshly ground black pepper and bring to the boil. Reduce the heat to a simmer and cook for 30 minutes, then strain through a fine sieve into a large measuring jug, discarding the solids.

Return the stock to the pan. You will need 6 cups (1.5 litres) stock, so add more water if necessary.

Stir in the sautéed leek mixture, along with the cauliflower and potato. Cover with a lid and bring to a simmer, then reduce the heat to medium–low and cook for 10 minutes, or until the vegetables are tender.

Using a slotted spoon, remove and reserve about 1 cup of the vegetables. Using a stick blender or upright blender, purée the remaining soup until smooth.

Stir in the remaining butter, then add the corn, white fish and prawns. Cook for 4 minutes, or until the seafood is just cooked through, then add the salmon and reserved vegetables, and warm for 1 minute.

Ladle the soup into serving bowls. Drizzle with a little extra oil and scatter with the parsley. Serve immediately, sprinkled with a pinch of extra paprika.

TOP TIPS

- **To speed things up, I chop and slice all the vegetables in a food processor.**
- **If you have some fresh or dried bay leaves, throw a couple of those in, too.**
- **For a dairy-free chowder, use olive oil instead of butter.**

HIGH IN PROTEIN LOW CARB

- Almost 1 serve protein per serve
- Great source of potassium + fibre
- Good source of folate
- No added sugars

QUICK 'N' EASY PHO Serves 4

Pho is considered Vietnam's national dish, and for good reason. The soup stock on which it is based usually takes many hours of patient simmering for the flavours to develop. This is my cheat's version, made with coconut water — my secret weapon. Coconut water varies in sweetness, so at the time of serving, check the flavours and balance them out to taste. Instead of beef, you can use shredded poached chicken. I suggest using beef stock if serving with beef, and chicken stock if using chicken. Or you can of course use mushroom stock for a vegan version, and omit the fish sauce.

1/2 SERVE VEG per serve

1 tablespoon neutral-flavoured oil, such as grapeseed or rice bran oil

4 red Asian or French shallots, thinly sliced

6 garlic cloves, crushed or finely chopped

2 tablespoons finely grated fresh ginger

2 cinnamon sticks

6 star anise

8 cloves

1 teaspoon fennel seeds

4 cups (1 litre) Beef stock (page 224), Chicken stock (page 220) or Mushroom stock (page 216)

1 litre (4 cups) pure unsweetened coconut water

4 dried shiitake mushrooms

175 g (6 oz) fried bean curd, sliced into matchsticks

3–4 tablespoons fish sauce (see tips)

200 g (7 oz) brown rice stick noodles

150 g (5½ oz) beef sirloin, very thinly sliced (see tips)

To serve

mixed herbs, such as Thai basil, Vietnamese mint, mint and coriander (cilantro)

bean sprouts

thinly sliced red chilli

lime wedges

Add the oil, shallot, garlic, ginger and spices to a large saucepan over medium–low heat. Once the oil starts to sizzle, cook for 5 minutes, or until fragrant, stirring regularly.

Add the stock, coconut water and dried mushrooms and bring to the boil, then reduce the heat and simmer for 30 minutes to soften the mushrooms and allow the flavours to infuse.

Strain the soup through a fine sieve, reserving the mushrooms and discarding the solids. Discard the woody stems, then thinly slice the mushrooms, or leave them whole. Return the broth and mushrooms to the pan. Stir in the bean curd and add the fish sauce to taste (see tip). Bring the broth back up to a simmer and cook for 5 minutes, or until heated through.

Meanwhile, prepare the noodles according to packet instructions. Divide among four serving bowls.

Ladle the soup into the bowls, then top with the mushrooms and beef.

Serve immediately, with the herbs, bean sprouts, chilli and lime wedges.

TOP TIPS

- The amount of fish sauce will depend on how seasoned your stock is and its depth of flavour. I use 4 tablespoons, but it's best to start at 3 tablespoons and taste it first. Don't forget there are noodles going into the soup, which are quite bland, so you definitely want to add enough flavour. Hoisin sauce is often served on the side, too.
- If using beef, be sure to slice it very thinly, as you're relying on the hot broth to cook it. Partially freezing the beef will make it easier to slice.

DIVIDE AND CONQUER

- Use the flavour-packed mushroom stock as a base and then the omnivores can add either beef or chicken to their bowls. Easy.

LOW SATURATED FAT

- Almost 2½ serves wholegrains per serve
- Almost 1½ serves protein per serve (if using beef)
- Good source of potassium and selenium
- Beef stock is a good source of vitamin B_{12}

MAKE AHEAD

You can make a double batch of the stock ahead of time. It will keep in an airtight container in the fridge for up to 3 days, or in the freezer for up to 6 months.

SLOPPY JOES Serves 4

Chips and cheese are the usual accompaniment to these hand-held marvels, but I feel there are so many good things in the bolognese sauce that nothing else is really necessary. Except for pickles, of course.

2¹/₂ SERVES VEG per serve

4 Milk buns (page 202)
½ quantity Bolognese sauce
(page 210)
sliced gherkins or pickles, to serve

Preheat the oven to 180°C (350°F). Wrap the buns individually in foil, place on a baking tray and heat in the oven for 5–10 minutes, or until warmed through.

Meanwhile, warm the bolognese sauce in a saucepan over medium heat for 5–10 minutes, stirring now and then.

To serve, cut the buns in half and top the bases with the bolognese sauce. Add some pickles, put the lids on and serve immediately.

TOP TIPS

- If you're feeding a crowd, use all 8 milk buns from page 202, and the full quantity of bolognese sauce, to serve 8 people. Of course, you can easily use store-bought milk buns for convenience.
- Warming the buns inside foil keeps them softer and prevents them drying out and becoming too crisp.
- To make the milk buns vegan, don't brush them with the egg yolk.

DIVIDE AND CONQUER

- When preparing the bolognese sauce, make two batches — one vegan, and the other using your choice of meat, making it easy to cater for both vegans and meat eaters. Serve the vegan sloppy joes with egg-free buns.

HEALTHY FATS

- Almost 1 serve protein per serve
- ½ serve legumes per serve

FISH BOWL Serves 4

This salad is a great way to get the kids to try new flavours, and is a hit with adults as well. For a gluten-free meal, use gluten-free flour and breadcrumbs in the fish patties, and use fish sauce or gluten-free soy sauce in the tangy Asian dressing.

**1
SERVE VEG
per serve**

2 tablespoons neutral-flavoured oil, such as grapeseed or rice bran oil

16 Fish patties (page 230), flattened into patties

200 g (7 oz) dried rice vermicelli noodles

1 quantity Tangy Asian dressing (page 195)

1 cup (100 g) bean sprouts

1 Lebanese cucumber, cut into long thin strips

1 large or 2 small celery stalks, thinly sliced on an angle

Vietnamese pickles (page 212), to taste

1 large handful of mixed herbs, such as mint, Vietnamese mint, coriander (cilantro) and Thai basil

Preheat the oven to 150°C (300°F). Line a tray with baking paper.

Heat half the oil in a large frying pan over medium heat. Cook half the fish patties for 3 minutes on each side, or until golden and cooked through, then transfer to the oven to keep warm. Heat the remaining oil and cook the remaining patties in the same way.

Meanwhile, prepare the noodles according to the packet instructions. Drain, place in a bowl and gently toss with half the dressing. Divide among four serving bowls.

Top the noodles with the patties, vegetables and herbs. Drizzle with the remaining dressing and serve.

DIVIDE AND CONQUER

- When making the patties, make half of them vegan. Use only half the fish, and an equal quantity of firm tofu, and combine in separate bowls with half the patty mixture, before shaping the two separate mixtures into patties. Cook the vegan patties first.

- With the tangy Asian dressing, either use soy sauce instead of fish sauce, or use half the soy sauce in half the dressing, and half the fish sauce in the remaining dressing.

**HIGH IN PROTEIN
LOW SATURATED FAT**

- 1 serve protein per serve
- 100% RDI vitamin B$_{12}$ + 20% RDI calcium (mainly in the fish and cucumber) per serve
- Good source of vitamin B$_3$

BANH MI — MY WAY
(see recipe pages 82–83)

BANH MI — MY WAY Serves 4

I would have to say this is my most-craved street 'snack'. While I've always found the processed luncheon meat component of the traditional Vietnamese rolls rather questionable, I just can't get past all the other wonderful flavours, so I feel this version is a happy compromise. Actually there are two versions below, one using store-bought bread rolls, and the other wrapped in home-made, gluten-free rice paper rolls. Both types are equally delicious — although you'll only need half the amount of filling ingredients with the gluten-free version. Why not try them both?

1¹/₂
SERVES VEG
per serve

Chicken liver pâté (page 234),
    for spreading
Mayo (page 192), for spreading
1 Lebanese cucumber, cut into batons
2 spring onions (scallions), quartered
    lengthways, then cut into 5 cm
    (2 inch) lengths
Vietnamese pickles (page 212), to taste
100 g (3½ oz) punnet of snow pea
    sprouts (optional), cut into thirds
4 tablespoons coarsely chopped
    coriander (cilantro)
gluten-free soy sauce or
    Maggi seasoning
thinly sliced red chilli (optional)

Traditional bread rolls
4 long crusty bread rolls

Gluten-free rolls
4 eggs
1 tablespoon gluten-free soy sauce
    or fish sauce
2 tablespoons neutral-flavoured oil,
    such as grapeseed or rice bran oil
8 large (22 cm/8½ inch) round rice
    paper sheets

If using traditional bread rolls, cut the rolls lengthways along the middle, without cutting all the way through. Spread the inside of each roll with pâté and mayonnaise. Stuff with the vegetables and herbs, then drizzle with soy sauce or seasoning. Sprinkle with chilli if using and serve.

For gluten-free rolls, whisk the eggs and soy sauce in a jug to combine. In a small non-stick frying pan — ideally one that is smaller than the diameter of the rice paper roll — heat 1 teaspoon of the oil over medium–high heat. Pour in one-eighth of the egg mixture and swirl the pan to cover the base. Cook for 30 seconds on each side, or until set. Remove and set aside on a plate while you cook the remaining egg mixture, adding another 1 teaspoon oil to the pan each time.

Half-fill a large bowl with cold water. Place a large piece of baking paper on a clean surface. Working one at a time, submerge a rice paper sheet into the water for 10 seconds, or until only just starting to soften. Place the rice paper sheet on the baking paper. Place an omelette round on top, then spread with pâté and mayo. Add only a little bit of the filling ingredients — you won't need as much as for the traditional rolls, and you won't be able to roll them up if you overfill them.

Take the side of the rice paper sheet that is closest to you and fold over one-third of the sheet to cover the filling, then rotate the sheet 90 degrees and begin to roll up to enclose, leaving the top open. Repeat with the remaining rice paper sheets and fillings and serve.

TOP TIPS

- If making the gluten-free rolls, don't leave the rice paper sheets in the water too long or they'll soften too much and fall apart. It's best to remove them from the water while they are still slightly stiff, as they'll continue to soften even once they're out of the water. This also means you won't need to mop up any excess water from the sheets.
- When cooking the omelettes for the gluten-free rolls, it's much easier to do this using a small frying pan that is just smaller than the diameter of the rice paper sheets.
- Traditionally, the spring onion and coriander are left whole or as a sprig, but I find they can be stringy and slide out of the rolls, so I like to chop them up for better flavour distribution. The same applies to the snow pea sprouts.

(see photo pages 80–81)

HEALTHY FATS

###

- ½ serve protein per serve
- 200% RDI vitamin B$_{12}$ per serve
- Good source of vitamin C, fibre, iron + betacarotene

MAKE AHEAD

If making the gluten-free rolls, you will have enough filling ingredients for 3–4 batches of rice paper rolls. You can assemble them several hours ahead and keep them covered in the fridge.

GNOCCHI TRAY BAKE Serves 4–6

Everyone in my family, including me, loves gnocchi, but if you've ever made it, you'll know it involves a bit of effort. It always pays off, of course, but I find this recipe is the perfect compromise, delivering all the flavour with minimal fuss. If you're dealing with a 'white food' obsession, the cauliflower and potato work well, and the spinach is cooked in the basil and tomato sauce, so it's definitely tasty enough — although you could also add the spinach to the gnocchi mixture. The white flecks in the cauliflower can even pass as ricotta!

just under
2¹/₂
SERVES VEG
per serve

1¾ cups (250 g) coarsely chopped cauliflower, or 250 g (9 oz) starchy/floury potatoes, peeled and coarsely chopped

1 tablespoon extra virgin olive oil, plus extra for drizzling

1¼ scant cups (200 g) fine semolina

scant ⅔ cup (150 g) fresh firm ricotta cheese

½ cup (50 g) finely grated parmesan or pecorino cheese

3 eggs

1 teaspoon fine sea salt

700 ml (24 fl oz) Roasted tomato passata (page 207) or store-bought tomato passata (puréed tomatoes)

250 g (9 oz) spinach or Swiss chard, finely shredded

1 large handful of basil, coarsely chopped

Preheat the oven to 180°C (350°F). Line a 30 × 20 cm (12 × 8 inch) baking tin with enough baking paper to overhang the sides, so you can lift out the gnocchi for ease of serving.

In a food processor, finely chop the cauliflower or potato, using a pulse action.

Bring the oil and 350 ml (12 fl oz) water to a simmer in a saucepan over medium heat. Gradually whisk in the semolina until combined. Using a wooden spoon, as best as you can, stir the mixture to combine — it will become lumpy very quickly. Transfer to a large bowl and leave until cool enough to handle. Add the cauliflower, ricotta and half the parmesan, then mix until well combined; it's easiest to use your hands for this. Mix in the eggs and salt until combined. Season with freshly ground black pepper to taste.

Transfer the mixture to the baking tin and evenly smooth out the surface using the back of a spoon. Bake for 35–40 minutes, or until set and lightly golden. Remove from the oven and leave to stand for 5 minutes before serving.

Near serving time, combine the passata, spinach and basil in a saucepan and cook over medium–low heat for 5 minutes, or until the sauce is hot and the spinach has wilted. Season to taste with salt and pepper. Keep warm over low heat.

Using the baking paper as handles, carefully lift the gnocchi bake from the baking tin, onto a chopping board, then cut into smaller shapes (I like diamonds).

Serve hot, drizzled with the tomato and spinach sauce and a little extra oil, and scattered with the remaining parmesan and salt and pepper to taste.

TOP TIPS
- Resist the urge to add more water to the pan when mixing in the semolina. The cauliflower or potato will release a lot of water during cooking, so it's best to keep the semolina at more of a dough-type consistency.
- If you don't have a food processor, don't chop the cauliflower or potato first. Instead, coarsely grate the cauliflower and potato from their whole state, using a box grater.

HEALTHY FATS

- ½ serve protein and ½ serve dairy per serve
- Over 50% RDI folate for adults per serve

MAKE AHEAD

You can make the gnocchi in advance. Remove from the oven as soon as it is lightly golden, wrap well and keep in the fridge for up to 3 days, or in an airtight container in the freezer for up to 3 months. Cut into pieces and gently pan-fry on both sides to serve.

VEGAN • DAIRY FREE • GLUTEN FREEABLE • NUT FREE • EGG FREE

'STEAK' SANDWICH Serves 4

Believe it or not, I gave one of these sandwiches to a meat-eating friend and he didn't even realise there was no meat in it — let alone that it was vegan! The thyme in the caramelised onions, the chunky tomato ketchup and the tangy mayo all contribute 'meaty' associations when tucking into this meat-free beauty.

just under
4
SERVES VEG
per serve

8 extra-large portobello or flat
   mushrooms, about 150 g (5½ oz)
   each, 'skins' peeled (see tip)
2 tablespoons olive oil, plus extra
   for drizzling
2–3 onions, thinly sliced into rounds
1 tablespoon thyme leaves

To assemble
8 large sourdough slices, or 4 rolls
   cut in half
Mayo (page 192)
rocket (arugula) leaves
Chunky tomato ketchup (page 226)

Preheat the grill (broiler) to high and line a baking tray with foil. Drizzle the mushrooms on both sides with oil and season with sea salt and freshly ground black pepper. Place the mushrooms on the baking tray and grill for 5 minutes on each side, or until golden and cooked.

If necessary, depending on the size and shape of your bread slices, cut the mushrooms so they'll fit into each sandwich properly.

Heat the 2 tablespoons olive oil in a large frying pan over medium–high heat. Add the onion and cook for 5 minutes, or until golden, stirring constantly. Reduce the heat to medium, add the thyme and cook for a further 2 minutes. Season with salt and pepper.

Lightly toast the bread if desired, or keep it fresh. Lightly spread mayo on each slice of bread, or inside the rolls. Divide the onion, rocket and mushroom steaks among the bottom halves, add a good dollop of chunky ketchup, put the lids on and serve immediately.

TOP TIP
- When grilling mushrooms, the thin outer layer or 'film' of skin on top of the mushroom caps can become a little chewy. You can simply peel off this thin layer, starting from the very outer edge of the mushroom cap — but don't discard it, as it is perfectly good to eat. If you do peel this outer layer off, the mushrooms will cook more quickly and will also burn more easily, so keep a close eye on them.
- For gluten-free sandwiches, use gluten-free bread.

**HEALTHY FATS
NO CHOLESTEROL**

✚
- About 50% RDI fibre per serve

VEGAN-ABLE • DAIRY FREE • GLUTEN FREEABLE • NUT FREE • EGG FREE

BLACK PEPPER TOFU AND PRAWNS

Serves 4

1¹/₂
SERVES VEG
per serve

This is my simplified, more affordable version of the beloved Singapore black pepper crab. The spiciness of the pepper is surprising — and addictive. For a more substantial meal, serve with brown rice or egg noodles.

1½ teaspoons each black and white peppercorns (or just black peppercorns), coarsely ground

2 garlic cloves, crushed

1 tablespoon finely grated fresh ginger

3 teaspoons maple syrup or raw sugar

2 tablespoons oyster sauce

2–4 teaspoons dark soy sauce, to taste

1 teaspoon cornflour

2½ tablespoons butter or coconut oil (or a combination)

175 g (6 oz) fried firm bean curd, sliced, or large tofu puffs, halved

125 g (4½ oz) snake beans or green beans, cut into 5 cm (2 inch) lengths

1 bunch broccolini, trimmed, cut into thirds

250 g (9 oz) choy sum, trimmed, stems and leaves separated, then cut into 5 cm (2 inch) lengths

400 g (14 oz) small raw prawns, peeled and deveined, tails left intact

In a small bowl, combine the pepper, garlic, ginger, maple syrup, oyster sauce and soy sauce. In another small bowl, mix the cornflour with 2 tablespoons water until smooth.

Melt half the butter in a wok or large deep frying pan over high heat. Add the bean curd, beans, broccolini and choy sum stems and stir-fry for 2 minutes.

Stir in the prawns and pepper sauce mixture. Give the cornflour mixture another quick stir until combined, then add to the pan and cook for a further minute. Add the choy sum leaves and stir-fry for a further minute.

Add the remaining butter and stir-fry for a further minute, until the prawns are cooked, and the vegetables are tender and warmed through.

TOP TIP
• For a gluten-free dish, use gluten-free oyster sauce and soy sauce.

DIVIDE AND CONQUER
• You can cook the prawns separately and add to individual plates at serving.
• For a vegan meal, omit the prawns and bump up the tofu, and use vegetarian oyster sauce.
• For a gluten-free dish, use gluten-free soy sauce and oyster sauce.

**HIGH IN PROTEIN
LOW CARB**

• 2 serves protein per serve
• 95% RDI vitamin C + 90% RDI folate per serve
• Good source of magnesium and iron

AIN'T-GOT-NO-BEEF STEAKS, MASH AND GRAVY Serves 4

8+
SERVES VEG
per serve

With the sheer variety of ingredients on offer these days, it can be a challenge to have every single meal perfectly balanced. A steak you order in a restaurant can be so massive it contains more red meat than should be consumed in an entire week! Flipping that idea, this recipe is all about getting the veg in, keeping in mind that you'll need to balance out your day with the other macronutrients you need. Oh, and the gravy really makes it.

2 heads of cauliflower
2 tablespoons olive oil
1 quantity of gravy, either Mushroom
    (page 217), Chicken (page 221)
    or Beef (page 225)
400 g (14 oz) green beans, trimmed

Roasted pumpkin mash
800 g (1 lb 12 oz) pumpkin or sweet
    potato, scrubbed well, cut into 2 cm
    (¾ inch) pieces
3 tablespoons extra virgin olive oil,
    or 1 tablespoon extra virgin olive oil
    and 2 tablespoons butter
    (or a combination)

Preheat the oven to 220°C (425°F). Line two large baking trays with baking paper.

To make the roasted pumpkin mash, spread the pumpkin or sweet potato on one of the baking trays, drizzle with 1 tablespoon oil and season with sea salt, tossing to coat. Cover with foil, then roast on the highest shelf of the oven for 10 minutes. Remove the foil and bake for a further 10–12 minutes, or until tender.

Meanwhile, turn the cauliflowers upside down, with the stalks facing upwards. What you want to do is cut two big 'steaks' from each one, each about 2 cm (¾ inch) thick, including some of the cauliflower inner core to hold the steaks together. It's easiest if you start along one side of the core and then carefully slice through the cauliflower so that the smaller, side florets will fall away, then cut through the middle of the core to make one steak. Repeat on the other side of the core to make a second steak, giving you two steaks from each cauliflower. Reserve the rest of the cauliflower to use in soups, curries, cauliflower 'rice' or White sauce (page 193), or steam and freeze in a zip-lock bag for up to 6 months.

Heat the 2 tablespoons olive oil in a large frying pan over medium–high heat. In two batches, cook the cauliflower steaks for 3 minutes on each side, until lightly golden, then transfer to the other baking tray. Roast for 15 minutes, or until tender.

When the pumpkin or sweet potato have finished roasting, place them in a saucepan over low heat with the 2 remaining tablespoons olive oil, or the butter. Mash and season to taste with salt and freshly ground black pepper. Keep warm.

Heat the gravy in a small saucepan over low heat until ready to serve.

Meanwhile, bring ½ cup (125 ml) salted water to the boil in a wide-based saucepan. Cook the beans for 3 minutes, or until tender, then drain.

Serve the cauliflower steaks immediately, with the mash, beans and gravy.

TOP TIPS
• Try stirring your favourite finely chopped herb into the mash.
• Instead of steaming the green beans, you can add them to the cauliflower roasting tray for the final 5 minutes of cooking, with a light drizzle of oil.
• For a vegan or dairy-free dish, use olive oil instead of butter in the gravy, and in the pumpkin mash. Also use mushroom gravy for the vegans.
• To make the dish gluten-free, use gluten-free flour in the gravy.

HEALTHY FATS

Great source of fibre, vitamin A, C and potassium

POUTINE TIME Serves 4

The first time I tried a proper poutine was in its Canadian homeland, in the ski-resort town of Whistler. Hot potato fries laden with thick warm gravy and clumps of cheese curd are irresistible in Canada's freezing winters — but your body will enjoy this make-at-home version much better, given it has only half the calories and carbs. If serving chicken stuffing with this recipe, you won't need to add the herbs.

6½
SERVES VEG
per serve

1.2 kg (2 lb 10 oz) root vegetables, such as sweet potato, parsnip, celeriac, potato and/or pumpkin, scrubbed or peeled

3 tablespoons neutral-flavoured oil, such as grapeseed or rice bran

1 quantity Gravy of your choice (see pages 217, 221, 223, 225)

½ quantity (600 ml) White sauce (page 193)

½ quantity Chicken stuffing (page 219), or about 200 g (7 oz) shredded poached or barbecued chicken (optional)

3 tablespoons finely chopped chives and/or parsley (optional)

Preheat the oven to 220°C (425°F). Line a large baking tray with baking paper.

Cut the vegetables into thick chips, cutting any potatoes smaller or more thinly as they take the longest to cook. Place the vegetables on the tray, drizzle with the oil and season well with sea salt and freshly ground black pepper, tossing to coat.

Spread the vegetables in a single layer and roast for 20 minutes, or until golden and cooked through.

Meanwhile, heat the gravy and white sauce in separate saucepans over low heat. Also warm the chicken stuffing or chicken, if using.

Serve the chips drizzled with the gravy and white sauce, scattered with the chicken and herbs, if using.

TOP TIPS

- To make the poutine gluten-free, use gluten-free flour and cornflour in the gravy.
- For a dairy-free or vegan meal, omit the cheese when making the white sauce, and use olive oil instead of butter.

DIVIDE AND CONQUER

- Simply serve with the gravy of your choice and add the chicken to individual serves.

HIGH IN PROTEIN

- 1 serve protein per serve
- 280% RDI vitamin C + over 80% RDI vitamin B_{12} per serve
- Great source of fibre

HONEST CHICKEN MEATBALL SOUP

Serves 4–6

just under
2
SERVES VEG
per serve

Pleasing all the troops should be easy with this super-simple soup. Feel free to change the vegetables, using chopped green beans, broccoli, corn and zucchini (courgettes) to mix it up.

8–10 cups (2–2.5 litres) Chicken stock (page 220), Mushroom stock (page 216), or good quality store-bought stock

6–8 baby carrots, scrubbed and sliced about 1 cm (½ inch) thick

1⅓ cups (120 g) short pasta, such as macaroni, ditalini or pasta shapes (see tip)

1 quantity Chicken meatballs (page 231)

1¾ cups (250 g) frozen peas, thawed

Pour the stock into a large saucepan and add the carrot.

Bring the stock to the boil, add the pasta and cook according to the packet instructions — adding the meatballs in the last 5 minutes of cooking, and the peas for the final 1 minute of cooking.

Serve the soup as soon as the pasta is al dente, and the meatballs and peas are cooked through.

TOP TIP
• This soup is a great opportunity to try the kids out on some interesting vegetable-based pastas that are increasingly becoming available.

HIGH IN PROTEIN

• Almost 1 serve wholegrains per serve
• ½ serve protein per serve
• Great source of vitamin B_3

CHAPTER THREE

DINNER TIME

LONG AND STRONG SOUP Serves 4

Wonton noodle soup — or 'long soup' as I grew up calling it — is a dish that has always been very close to me. My mum would often pick up a few of these soups from our local Chinese for us to share and enjoy after school. Sadly, that restaurant is long gone, so by making it at home, I feel I can introduce it to my daughter and carry on the tradition.

1¹/₂ SERVES VEG per serve

375 g (13 oz) fresh egg noodles

24 uncooked pork dumplings, made using the Pork dumpling balls mixture on page 233, and the dumplings recipe on page 21

8 cups (2 litres) Chicken stock (page 220) or Mushroom stock (page 216)

soy sauce, to taste (optional)

1 bunch broccolini or Chinese broccoli, cut into 5 cm (2 inch) lengths

225 g (8 oz) tin bamboo shoots (optional), drained and rinsed well (see tip)

2 zucchini (courgettes), shredded into thin noodles (zoodles)

1 handful of garlic chives, cut into 4 cm (1½ inch) lengths

1–2 teaspoons sesame oil

Bring a large saucepan of water to the boil. Cook the noodles according to the packet instructions, then remove with tongs and divide among serving bowls.

Return the water to a simmer, add the dumplings and cook for 3–5 minutes, gently stirring the water occasionally, until the dumplings rise to the surface. Remove with a slotted spoon and divide among the serving bowls.

Meanwhile, in another large saucepan, bring the stock to a simmer, seasoning to taste with soy sauce or sea salt, or a combination of the two. Add the broccolini and bamboo shoots and simmer for 2 minutes, then add the zucchini and chives and simmer for 1 minute.

Ladle the soup among the serving bowls, drizzle with the sesame oil and serve.

TOP TIPS

- Some brines can be a little overpowering, so I steep the tinned bamboo shoots in boiling water for 5 minutes to remove the flavour.
- I cook the greens in with the stock, rather than with the noodles, so any nutrients that leach into the water are captured in the soup, rather than tipped down the drain. However, the dumplings are best cooked in water, rather than the stock, as they will make the stock starchy and murky.

DIVIDE AND CONQUER

- Use mushroom stock as the base of the soup. Prepare some vegan dumplings, following the tip in the dumplings recipe on page 21, and make the rest using pork. Cook the vegan dumplings first in the boiling water, then cook the pork dumplings, serving them separately.

**HEALTHY FATS
HIGH IN PROTEIN**

✚

½ serve protein per serve

BUTTER-NUT CHICKEN Serves 4

Butter chicken is one of the most searched recipes online to cook and enjoy at home. My version below has far less chicken than your average butter chicken, but is still high in protein, containing 60 per cent of the recommended daily intake for women in every serve, and 50 per cent for men — with half the protein coming from plant sources. The pumpkin gives the sauce a lovely sweetness, and using the home-made, yoghurt-based Sour-ish cream on page 192 means you don't need to add saturated fat–laden cream, and can keep the butter to a minimum, too.

just under
3
SERVES VEG
per serve

2–3 long red chillies, coarsely chopped

1 tablespoon garam masala

4 cm (1½ inch) knob of fresh ginger, peeled and coarsely chopped

1 teaspoon fine sea salt

200 g (7 oz/¾ cup) Sour-ish cream (page 192)

300 g (10½ oz) boneless, skinless chicken thighs, trimmed and cut into 2.5 cm (1 inch) chunks

250 g (9 oz) peeled and seeded butternut pumpkin

500 g (1 lb 2 oz) cauliflower

½ cup (50 g) almond meal

400 ml (14 fl oz) Roasted tomato passata (page 207), or store-bought tomato passata (puréed tomatoes); see tips

1 tablespoon butter

¾ cup (150 g) brown or white basmati rice

½ cup (75 g) blanched almonds, lightly toasted

mint and/or coriander (cilantro) leaves, to serve

Using a stick blender, blender or small food processor, blend the chillies, garam masala, ginger and salt to the smoothest possible paste.

Transfer the spice paste to a cold saucepan and stir in the sour-ish cream until well combined. Mix the chicken pieces through and leave to marinate while you prepare the remaining vegetables.

Coarsely grate half the pumpkin into a bowl, and cut the remainder into 2 cm (¾ inch) pieces. Finely chop the cauliflower, by hand or using a food processor.

Add the grated and chopped pumpkin to the chicken, along with the almond meal and passata, and stir to combine. Place over medium heat, then cover and cook for 20 minutes, or until the chicken is cooked and the pumpkin is tender, stirring occasionally. Add the butter and stir until melted, then season to taste with sea salt. For a thinner consistency, stir in 3–4 tablespoons water if desired.

Meanwhile, bring a saucepan of salted water to the boil. If using brown basmati rice, cook the rice for 10 minutes, then add the cauliflower and cook for a further 10 minutes, or until the rice and cauliflower are tender. If using white basmati rice, add the cauliflower at the same time as the rice and cook them together for 10 minutes, or until tender. Drain.

Serve the curry with the rice, scattered with the almonds and herbs.

TOP TIPS

- If using a food processor to chop up the cauliflower, be careful not to take it too far, or too much water will leach out of the cauliflower, making your rice lumpy and soft. You can avoid this by chopping by hand.
- Chillies can be hotter at different times of the year, so if you're more inclined to eat milder curries, use only two chillies.
- If using store-bought passata, see the recipe note on page 207.

DIVIDE AND CONQUER

- For a vegetarian curry, replace the chicken with an extra 1 cup (125 g) cauliflower florets, and/or a drained 400 g (14 oz) tin of chickpeas. Or to cook the chicken separately, place on a foil-lined grill (broiler) tray, season with salt and grill under high heat for 8–10 minutes, until cooked through.

**HEALTHY FATS
HIGH IN PROTEIN**

- 2 serves wholegrains + 1.5 serves protein per serve
- Great source of fibre and vitamin C

DAIRY FREE • GLUTEN FREE • NUT FREE • EGG FREE

PULLIN' PORK TACOS Serves 4

There really isn't any need to fill a taco with heaps of meat. Loaded with protein, these tacos are the meatiest 'lesser meat' tacos you'll ever make. They are such a tasty way to enjoy a variety of healthy veg, topped off with a zingy cabbage and pineapple salsa and creamy avocado. Another bonus is that you can prepare the pulled pork several days in advance to save time: the flavours will only get better.

3½
SERVES VEG
per serve

Pulled pork

400 g (14 oz) pork scotch fillet steaks, thickly sliced

½ cup (110 g) dried black beans

1 corn cob, kernels removed

1 red capsicum (pepper), cut into 1 cm (½ inch) pieces

400 ml (14 fl oz) Roasted tomato passata (page 207), or store-bought tomato passata (puréed tomatoes); see tip

½ cup (125 ml) orange juice

4 tablespoons apple cider vinegar or white vinegar

1–2 chipotle chillies in adobo sauce (see tip); alternatively, use 1–2 tablespoons finely chopped pickled jalapeño chillies and 2 teaspoons smoked paprika

2 teaspoons dried oregano

1 teaspoon ground cumin or toasted cumin seeds

To serve

2 cups (150 g) finely shredded red cabbage

juice of 1 lime

12 corn tortillas

½ cup (100 g) finely chopped pineapple

4 tablespoons finely chopped coriander (cilantro)

1 avocado, cut into 1 cm (½ inch) pieces

Place all the pulled pork ingredients in a saucepan, add 1½ cups (375 ml) water and bring to a simmer over medium heat. Cover with a lid, reduce the heat to medium–low and cook for 45 minutes.

Meanwhile, put the cabbage and lime juice in a non-metallic bowl and leave to lightly pickle.

Remove the lid from the pork and cook, uncovered, for a further 30 minutes, or until the pork and beans are tender, adding more water as needed (just ¼ cup at a time: you don't want the mixture to be too wet).

Just before serving, warm the tortillas, according to the packet instructions.

Using two forks, shred the pork, then season the mixture to taste with sea salt.

Lightly season the cabbage with salt, mixing in the pineapple and coriander.

Serve the tortillas with the pulled pork mixture, cabbage salsa and avocado.

TOP TIPS

- If using store-bought passata, add 1 finely chopped red onion and 2 finely chopped garlic cloves.
- Be careful not to season the pulled pork mixture with salt until the very end, when the black beans are cooked, otherwise they will remain tough and will refuse to soften.
- If you prefer, you can cook the pulled pork in a casserole dish in a preheated 150°C (300°F) oven, following the same process as above.
- Chipotle chillies in adobo sauce can be rather spicy, so adjust the quantity to suit your taste.

HEALTHY FATS
HIGH IN PROTEIN

- Over 1.5 serves protein per serve
- 1 serve legumes per serve
- Great source of iron, fibre, vitamin C and folate

MAKE AHEAD

You can easily make a double batch of pulled pork and freeze it in an airtight container for up to 3 months.

BUFFALO HOT THINGS Serves 4

'Buffalo wings' are delicious, of course — but why does it need to be all about the chicken? Sure, throw in a few chicken wings, but round it all out with a colourful array of sweet roasted vegetables, which taste truly wonderful doused in this spicy, buttery sauce. I find this makes a good party tray, too!

**6¹⁄₂
SERVES VEG
per serve**

4–6 organic chicken wings, jointed; reserve the wing tips for the Chicken stock on page 220

2 corn cobs, husks and silks removed, then quartered crossways into 'wheels'

¼ jap or kent pumpkin, seeds removed, cut into large wedges

300 g (10½ oz) sweet potato, washed well and thickly sliced

2 red capsicums (peppers), cut into flat 'cheeks'

2 red onions, cut into wedges

hot sauce, to serve (optional)

Hot buffalo sauce

2 garlic cloves, peeled

a pinch of sea salt

3 tablespoons butter

½ cup (125 ml) hot sauce, such as Frank's or Cholula

1 teaspoon maple syrup or raw sugar

Preheat the oven to 220°C (425°F) fan-forced. Line a large baking tray with baking paper.

While the oven is heating, make the hot buffalo sauce. Place the garlic on a chopping board and sprinkle with the salt. Crush the garlic to a paste using the blade of a knife, then place the crushed garlic in a small saucepan. Add the butter and allow to melt over medium heat. Whisk in the hot sauce and maple syrup until combined, then set aside.

Spread the chicken and all the vegetables on the baking tray. Drizzle the hot buffalo sauce over, season well with salt and toss until well coated. Spread out all the ingredients in a single layer and roast for 30 minutes, or until the chicken wings and vegies are golden and cooked through.

Serve immediately, with extra hot sauce if desired.

TOP TIP

- There is no need to peel the pumpkin and sweet potato. There's a load of healthy fibre in the skin, which is perfectly edible.

DIVIDE AND CONQUER

- You can bake the chicken on a separate tray, reserving some of the buttery sauce to coat the wings. Or, to keep it totally vegetarian, swap the chicken for about 250 g (9 oz) mushrooms, and make an extra half a batch of the sauce to nicely coat all the vegetables.

- ½ serve protein per serve
- Over 50% RDI fibre + 33% adult RDI folate per serve
- High in antioxidants, vitamin C and betacarotene

THAT'S SOME SATAY CURRY Serves 4

You can't beat the flavours of satay, with its peanut-based sauce. It feels like only yesterday that guilt trips were laid on us for eating 'fatty' foods such as nuts, but thankfully the benefits of healthy fats are becoming more widely appreciated, so you don't need to feel guilty about hooking into this satisfying curry. As well as healthy fats, peanuts are also an excellent source of protein. Despite the lesser amount of chicken in this recipe, it still offers a whopping 2 serves of protein in every serve. On average, women need around 2½ serves and men 3 serves of protein per day.

2 SERVES VEG per serve

250 g (9 oz) short-grain brown rice

1 tablespoon coconut oil, or a neutral-flavoured oil

250–400 g (9–14 oz) boneless, skinless chicken thighs, trimmed, cut into 3 cm (1¼ inch) chunks

3–4 tablespoons Malaysian-style curry powder (see tip)

1 carrot, peeled and coarsely chopped, or 1 yellow, red or green capsicum (pepper), chopped

3 cups (350 g) small cauliflower florets

400 ml (14 fl oz) coconut milk

½ cup (140 g) good-quality peanut or other nut butter, crunchy or smooth

150 g (5½ oz) green beans, trimmed and cut into 2 cm (¾ inch) lengths

2 cups (100 g) baby English spinach leaves

2 teaspoons finely grated palm sugar (jaggery), or 2 teaspoons raw sugar or maple syrup

3 tablespoons gluten-free soy sauce

1 tablespoon lime juice

coriander (cilantro), to serve (optional)

Bring a saucepan filled with plenty of water to the boil. Add the rice and cook for 25 minutes, or until tender. Drain and keep warm.

Meanwhile, heat the oil in a large deep frying pan over medium heat. Add the chicken and curry powder and cook, stirring, for 2 minutes, until fragrant.

Stir in the carrot, cauliflower, coconut milk, peanut butter and 3 tablespoons water. Cover with a lid and reduce the heat to low, then cook for 8 minutes, stirring occasionally.

Stir in the beans, giving the pan another good stir to stop the curry sticking to the bottom. Cover and cook for a further 10 minutes, then add the spinach, sugar and soy sauce, stirring for 1 minute, or until the spinach has wilted. Turn off the heat and stir in the lime juice to combine.

Serve the curry immediately, with the brown rice.

TOP TIPS

- Curry powders vary in strength, so check the packet recommendations as a guide to the amount to use.
- If the curry is a little too thick, stir in 1 tablespoon water at a time until you reach the desired consistency.
- If you'd like the cauliflower broken down a little more to disguise it, add it at the same time as the chicken. Or, instead of adding the cauliflower to the curry, you could serve the curry with cauliflower 'rice'.

DIVIDE AND CONQUER

- If you would like to serve the chicken as a separate meal, fry it in a separate small frying pan for about 6 minutes, turning now and then, until golden and cooked. Toast the curry powder in the oil on its own.
- To boost the vegetables for vegetarians, you can add chopped capsicum (pepper) and carrot, or add more spinach leaves.

HIGH IN PROTEIN

- 3½ serves wholegrains + 2 serves protein per serve
- Over 100% RDI niacin (from peanut butter) + 60% RDI magnesium (mainly from rice and cauliflower) + 50% RDI folate (mainly from peanut butter and cauliflower) per serve
- Great source of fibre, folate and vitamins B_3, E and C

MAKE AHEAD
The curry can be frozen in an airtight container for up to 3 months.

ROASTED TOMATO RISOTTO

Serves 4 as risotto | Serves 6 with meatballs

**2
SERVES VEG
per serve**

Risottos can be rather demanding of your time and attention, with all that constant stirring and hovering over the pan. But not this risotto. It is the easiest and most delicious risotto I've ever made for my family. I throw it into the oven and go and do more pressing things — such as sitting down for a few moments! I often serve this risotto with Chicken meatballs (page 231). You can fry them separately in a frying pan over medium heat for 6–8 minutes, until cooked and golden, or add them to the risotto after it has been baking in the oven for 15 minutes.

1 tablespoon olive oil

2 small carrots, scrubbed or peeled, thinly sliced on an angle

1⅓ cups (300 g) arborio rice

400 ml (14 fl oz) Roasted tomato passata (page 207), or a 400 g (14 oz) tin chopped tomatoes

3 cups (750 ml) hot Chicken stock (page 220) or Mushroom stock (page 216)

¾ cup (150 g) finely chopped roasted red capsicum (pepper)

250 g (9 oz) cherry tomatoes

⅓ cup (30 g) finely grated parmesan cheese

coarsely chopped basil or parsley, to serve

1 quantity Chicken meatballs (page 231); optional (see tips)

Preheat the oven to 200°C (400°F).

Heat the oil in a large flameproof casserole dish over medium–high heat. Cook the carrot for 1 minute, then stir in the rice and cook for 1 minute, or until the rice is well coated in the oil.

Stir in the passata, stock, capsicum and cherry tomatoes. Season well with sea salt and freshly ground black pepper and bring to a simmer.

Cover with a lid, transfer to the oven and bake for 20 minutes, or until the rice is al dente and most of the liquid has been absorbed. Stir in half the parmesan.

Set aside to rest, covered, for 5 minutes.

Serve scattered with the herbs and remaining parmesan.

TOP TIPS

- If you'd like the chicken meatballs to be gluten free, replace the burghul with a finely chopped vegetable such as broccoli or cauliflower, or with ½ cup (60 g) gluten-free flour such as chickpea (besan) or buckwheat.
- To cook the meatballs, you can fry them in a frying pan over medium heat for 6–8 minutes, until cooked and golden, or add them to the risotto after it has been baking in the oven for 15 minutes.

DIVIDE AND CONQUER

- For a vegan risotto, use mushroom stock, and omit the cheese and meatballs, or serve with the Vego balls on page 227.
- For omnivores, cook and serve the chicken meatballs separately.

HEALTHY FATS

- 1 serve wholegrains + ½ serve protein per serve
- 50% RDI selenium per serve
- Great source of fibre, and vitamins C, B_3 and B_{12}

VEGO-ABLE • GLUTEN FREEABLE • NUT FREE • EGG FREE

MUSHROOM STROGANOFF WITH BEEF Serves 4

When I was a kid, beef stroganoff was the dish I'd ask for most often. Mum always served it with rice, hence my choice here, but stroganoff is typically served with pasta, such as fettuccine, so use whichever you prefer. (I think black rice is a great wholegrain choice, and looks pretty cool on the plate, too!) Until about the age of ten I really didn't like mushrooms because of their slippery texture, but when I came around to them, I would look for them in my first mouthfuls of stroganoff – I always had mainly beef left at the end, as I had eaten all the mushrooms, rice and sauce! So here, mushrooms, rather than beef, are the hero. A traditional stroganoff for four would use around 800 g (1 lb 12 oz) beef, rather than the 250 g (9 oz) here, which means that in that one meal you would be consuming 100% of the daily protein intake recommended for men. A traditional strog also has more calories, more saturated fat, and only half the veg of this version.

just under
3
SERVES VEG
per serve

1¼ cups (250 g) black or brown rice
2 tablespoons olive oil
250 g (9 oz) rump steak, trimmed, thinly sliced
1 tablespoon butter
1 onion, finely chopped
800 g (1 lb 12 oz) mushrooms, such as Swiss brown, or a combination, thinly sliced or quartered
3 teaspoons sweet paprika
400 ml (14 fl oz) Roasted tomato passata (page 207), or store-bought tomato passata (puréed tomatoes)
1 cup (275 g) Sour-ish cream (page 192)
1 tablespoon Worcestershire sauce (optional; see tip)
finely chopped parsley, to serve (optional)

In a saucepan, bring plenty of water to the boil. Add the rice and cook for 25 minutes, or until tender. Drain and keep warm.

Meanwhile, heat 1 tablespoon of the oil in a large deep frying pan over high heat. Cook the beef for 2 minutes, stirring, until lightly golden. Season with sea salt and freshly ground black pepper, then remove to a bowl.

Reduce the heat to medium–high. Add the butter and onion and cook, stirring, for 1 minute, then add half the mushrooms. Cook for 5 minutes, or until golden, stirring often, then transfer to a bowl.

Heat the remaining 1 tablespoon oil in the pan. Cook the remaining mushrooms for 5 minutes, or until golden, stirring often.

Return all the mushroom mixture to the pan. Sprinkle with the paprika, season with salt and pepper and cook for 1 minute. Stir in the passata, sour-ish cream, and Worcestershire sauce. Cook for 2 minutes, then return the beef to the pan and cook for a further 1 minute, or until heated through.

Serve the stroganoff with the rice, scattered with parsley if you like.

TOP TIP
• To make the dish gluten-free, omit the worcestershire sauce.

DIVIDE AND CONQUER
• To make the dish vegetarian, omit the beef and Worcestershire sauce, and bump the mushrooms up to 1 kg (2 lb 4 oz). For those who would like beef, cook up a bit less separately, and add it into individual serves upon serving.

**HEALTHY FATS
HIGH IN PROTEIN**

• 3.5 serves wholegrains + 1 serve protein per serve
• Great source of niacin (mostly from mushrooms), which can help improve cholesterol levels
• Great source of selenium + fibre

TASTY TACO SALAD Serves 4

I usually can't go past a taco salad on a menu — but it doesn't have to be laden with cheese, sour cream and deep-fried corn chips to taste great. This feel-good sibling will do the trick.

1¹/₂ SERVES VEG per serve

6 corn tortillas, thinly sliced

1 tablespoon olive oil, plus extra for drizzling

250 g (9 oz) lean minced beef, or beef stir-fry strips

400 g (14 oz) tin beans, such as black, pinto or kidney beans, drained well

1 tablespoon Mexican spice mix (see tip)

1 ripe avocado

juice of 1 small lime, or to taste

1 tablespoon finely chopped coriander (cilantro)

¾ cup (75 g) finely grated haloumi

½ iceberg lettuce, finely shredded

4 radishes (optional), shaved or shredded

½ cup (135 g) Sour-ish cream (page 192)

Tomato salsa

250 g (9 oz) tomatoes, halved, seeds removed, finely chopped

2 tablespoons finely chopped coriander (cilantro) stems

½ small red onion or 1 French shallot, finely chopped

2–4 tablespoons finely chopped pickled jalapeño chillies

1 tablespoon lime juice

Preheat the oven to 180°C (350°F). Line a large baking tray with baking paper.

Spread the tortilla strips on the baking tray and lightly drizzle with oil. Lightly season with sea salt, toss to coat, then arrange in a single layer. Bake for 8–10 minutes, or until golden and crisp. Remove from the oven and allow to cool.

Meanwhile, combine all the tomato salsa ingredients in a bowl. Season with salt and set aside until ready to serve.

Heat the 1 tablespoon of oil in a frying pan over medium–high heat. Cook the beef, beans and spice mix for 5 minutes, stirring regularly, until the beef has browned. Season with salt.

Meanwhile, scoop the avocado flesh into a bowl and mash with the lime juice. Season with sea salt and stir the coriander through to combine.

Combine the haloumi with the tortilla strips.

Divide the beef mixture among serving bowls. Top with the lettuce and radish, if using. Serve immediately, with the sour-ish cream, avocado, tomato salsa and the cheesy tortilla strips.

TOP TIP

- There are many different spice mixes available, varying in heat and strength, so bear this in mind when flavouring the dish.
- For a dairy-free version, omit the haloumi and sour-ish cream.

DIVIDE AND CONQUER

- You can make this salad pescatarian by using raw peeled prawns instead of beef and frying them off with just 1 teaspoon Mexican spice mix — or even just use cooked prawns, which will not require cooking at all. If using prawns, I'd definitely add the radish, as they taste great together.
- For a vegan salad, add another tin of beans and omit the beef or prawns, as well as the haloumi and sour-ish cream.
- To go half vegetarian, cook the beef or prawns separately with half the spice mix, then add them to individual plates on serving.

**HEALTHY FATS
HIGH IN PROTEIN**

- Over 1 serve protein + ½ serve legumes per serve
- 50% RDI folate + 25% RDI calcium per serve

VEGAN-ABLE • DAIRY FREE • GLUTEN FREEABLE • NUT FREE • EGG FREE

CHICK CHICK CACCIATORE Serves 4

Chicken cacciatore is one of those family favourites everyone seems to like. Here I've ramped up the veg and turned it into a one-pan wonder complete with risoni pasta and chickpeas — and lots of antioxidants, too. You can omit the anchovies, if desired, but they do add a lovely depth of flavour.

3
SERVES VEG
per serve

2 garlic cloves, peeled

4 anchovy fillets

2 tablespoons olive oil

250–400 g (9–14 oz) boneless, skinless free-range chicken thighs, trimmed, cut into 3 cm (1¼ inch) cubes

2 celery stalks, thinly sliced

1 red capsicum (pepper), cut into 2 cm (¾ inch) pieces

3 cups (750 ml) Chicken stock (page 220)

400 ml (14 fl oz) Roasted tomato passata (page 207), or store-bought tomato passata (puréed tomatoes); see tips

1⅓ cups (300 g) risoni

400 g (14 oz) tin chickpeas, drained well

⅔ cup (100 g) pitted kalamata olives

200 g (7 oz) green beans, trimmed and halved

4 tablespoons oregano, basil or parsley leaves

Finely chop the garlic and anchovies together on a board. Set aside.

Heat 1 tablespoon of the oil in a large saucepan over medium–high heat. Cook the chicken for 3 minutes, turning now and then, until lightly golden all over. Remove the chicken to a bowl.

Heat the remaining 1 tablespoon oil in the pan, then cook the garlic and anchovy mixture for 1 minute, stirring often. Add the celery and capsicum and sauté for a further 2 minutes.

Stir in the stock and the passata and bring to the boil. Add the risoni and return the chicken and any juices to the pan. Cook for 5 minutes, giving everything a good stir to stop the risoni sticking to the bottom of the pan.

Stir in the chickpeas, olives and beans and cook for a further 5 minutes, or until the risoni is al dente.

Stir in the herbs and serve.

TOP TIPS

- If using store-bought passata, add 1 finely chopped red onion and fry it with the garlic and anchovy mixture.
- For a gluten-free dish, instead of risoni use 750 g (1 lb 10 oz) chopped potatoes, cut into bite-sized pieces.

DIVIDE AND CONQUER

- You can easily make this dish vegan, by omitting the anchovies and adding a second tin of chickpeas if desired. You can cook the chicken separately for the omnivores.

HEALTHY FATS
HIGH IN PROTEIN

- 1 serve protein + ½ serve legumes per serve
- Great source of fibre
- Great source of iron + vitamins B_3, C and E

SPANISH TORTILLA QUICHE Serves 4

I like bringing two classics together, to enjoy the best of both worlds. Here, one of Spain's national dishes, the tortilla, meets one of France's most popular, the quiche: European fusion at its finest. But with tofu, you ask? It may not sound overly appealing, but silken tofu really does give a boost of nutritious creaminess in this dish, without all the saturated fat of cream. And there are certainly not as many serves of veg in your traditional quiche lorraine, as there is in this one.

2½ SERVES VEG per serve

1 quantity My shortcrust pastry (page 204), chilled

2½ tablespoons butter, plus extra for greasing

2 red onions, halved and thinly sliced

2 garlic cloves, thinly sliced or crushed

300 g (10½ oz) potatoes, scrubbed, then sliced as thinly as possible, about 2 mm (1/16 inch) thick

1 tablespoon thyme leaves

300 g (10½ oz) organic silken tofu, drained

4 eggs

½ cup (50 g) finely grated parmesan cheese

100 g (3½ oz) cherry tomatoes, left whole

smoked paprika, for sprinkling

green salad, to serve

Preheat the oven to 180°C (350°F). Lightly grease a 24 cm x 3 cm fluted quiche dish or tin.

On a clean work surface, roll out the pastry to about 3 mm (⅛ inch) thick, large enough to line the base and side of the quiche dish. Ease the pastry into the dish and trim the edges. Using a fork, prick holes in the base. Scrunch up a large piece of baking paper and use it to line the pastry base. Chill in the freezer until the oven reaches temperature.

Half-fill the dish with baking beads or dried pulses. Bake the pastry for 15 minutes, then carefully remove the baking paper and baking beads and bake for a further 10 minutes to dry out the base.

Meanwhile, in a large deep frying pan, brown the butter over medium heat until it is golden brown and has a nutty aroma, swirling the pan. Add the onion and garlic and cook for 3 minutes, or until starting to soften. Add the potatoes and most of the thyme and partially cover with a lid. Cook for 6–8 minutes, stirring occasionally, until the potatoes are slightly tender. Turn off the heat and stand, covered, until ready to use.

Using a stick blender, blend the tofu, eggs and most of the parmesan in a large bowl. Season well with sea salt and freshly ground black pepper. Add the potato mixture and stir until combined.

Transfer the mixture to the pastry base and smooth the surface. Arrange the tomatoes on top, and scatter with the remaining thyme and parmesan. Season with salt and pepper and sprinkle well with paprika. Bake for 25–30 minutes, or until the pastry is golden and cooked, and the filling is set.

Remove from the oven and rest for 10 minutes, then serve with a green salad.

TOP TIP

- When blind-baking pastry, it is better to use either baking beads or dried pulses (such as kidney beans) rather than dried rice, to allow the heat to properly get through to the pastry base and dry it out.

HIGH IN PROTEIN

- Almost 1½ serves protein per serve
- ½ serve legumes per serve
- Over 50% RDI vitamin C per serve
- Good source of fibre
- Tofu is a source of iron

MAKE AHEAD

You can make the quiche a few hours in advance and gently reheat in the oven for serving.

SPAGHETTI 'N' MORE MEATBALLS Serves 4

Only recently I discovered that spaghetti meatballs are actually an American invention, rather than Italian, as I'd long imagined. Such a successful combination, this dish always goes down well. It is also wonderfully versatile, as you can easily cater for different tastes by serving the spaghetti with different types of meatballs or vegie balls. Without losing out on carbs, this version serves up a bit less pasta, adding in zucchini noodles for a healthy veg and 'pasta' boost.

2¹/₂
SERVES VEG
per serve

250 g (9 oz) wholemeal or gluten-free spaghetti

2 tablespoons extra virgin olive oil, plus extra for drizzling

1 quantity Beef, lamb, or veal and pork meatballs (page 232), or Vego balls (page 227)

2 large zucchini (courgettes)

400 ml (14 fl oz) Roasted tomato passata (page 207), or store-bought tomato passata (puréed tomatoes)

finely grated parmesan cheese, to serve (optional)

Bring a saucepan of salted water to the boil and cook the pasta according to the packet instructions. Drain, reserving ½ cup (125 ml) of the pasta water.

Meanwhile, heat half the oil in a large deep frying pan over medium heat. Working in batches, cook the meatballs or vego balls for 8–10 minutes, or until golden and cooked through. Remove to a bowl.

Slice lengthways around each zucchini, leaving the seeds in the centre, then cut the seedy bits into 1 cm (½ inch) chunks. Cut the edges into zucchini noodles or 'zoodles'. (Alternatively, use a julienne peeler or spiraliser if you have one.)

Heat the remaining oil in the pan over medium heat. Cook the zucchini chunks for 1 minute, then add the zoodles and pasta and cook, stirring, for about 1 minute.

Stir in the passata and reserved pasta water, along with the meatballs, and cook for a further 2 minutes, or until heated through.

Drizzle with a little more olive oil and serve scattered with grated parmesan, if desired.

TOP TIP

- Pulse-based pastas make a great gluten-free alternative to regular durum wheat pasta.

HEALTHY FATS
HIGH IN PROTEIN

- Almost 3 serves wholegrains per serve
- 1 serve protein per serve
- High in fibre
- Great source of iron + vitamins B_{12} and C

TOAD IN THE HOLE Serves 4

This is my take on a beloved age-old classic, with braised lamb standing in for the sausages that are traditionally nestled in a Yorkshire pudding batter. The lamb may be secondary in terms of quantity, but certainly not in flavour.

3
SERVES VEG
per serve

2 parsnips, peeled or scrubbed, quartered, cores removed, then halved crossways

8 baby carrots, scrubbed, or 2 large carrots, peeled and thickly sliced

olive oil, for drizzling

1 quantity braised lamb, from the Lamb stock recipe on page 222 (see tip)

1 quantity Lamb gravy (page 223) or Chicken gravy (page 221)

250 g (9 oz) sugar snap peas

1⅔ cups (250 g) frozen peas

2 tablespoons finely chopped mint (optional)

Yorkshire pudding

200 ml (7 fl oz) milk

200 ml (7 fl oz) eggs (about 4)

¾ cup (125 g) plain flour

4 tablespoons olive oil

To make the Yorkshire pudding, whisk the milk and eggs in a large bowl to combine. Whisk in the flour until smooth. Season with sea salt, then strain through a fine sieve into a jug. Leave to rest in the fridge for about 20 minutes while heating the oven and oil.

Heat the oven to 220°C (425°F). Line a large baking tray with baking paper.

Pour the oil into a 20 cm (8 inch) solid cake tin. (Make sure you don't use a loose-based or spring-form tin, as the oil will seep through, creating a fire hazard in the oven.) Place the cake tin on a higher shelf in the oven for 5–10 minutes, or until the oil is very hot.

Meanwhile, put the parsnips and carrots on the baking tray. Drizzle with oil, season with sea salt and freshly ground black pepper and toss to coat.

With this next step, you'll need to work quite quickly, because you want to keep the oil and the oven as hot as possible for a beautifully puffed Yorkshire pudding; leaving the oven door open too long will allow too much heat escape. Working quickly, very carefully pour the pudding mixture into the hot oil in the cake tin. Place the tray of vegetables on a lower shelf and close the oven door. Reduce the oven temperature to 200°C (400°F) and bake for 20–25 minutes, or until the pudding and vegetables are golden and cooked.

Meanwhile, mix the lamb and gravy together in a saucepan and gently warm over low heat. Keep warm.

Bring ½ cup (125 ml) salted water to the boil in a small saucepan with a lid. Add the sugar snap peas to the pan and steam with the lid on for 2 minutes, then add the frozen peas and cook for a further 1 minute, or until tender and heated through. Drain.

Transfer the Yorkshire pudding to a warm serving platter. Using a slotted spoon, spoon the lamb into the base of the pudding. Pour the gravy over and serve immediately, with the peas and mint, if using.

TOP TIP

- Instead of braised lamb, you can use a 250 g (9 oz) lamb backstrap fillet. Heat 1 tablespoon oil in a frying pan over medium–high heat. Season the lamb with salt and pepper and cook for 2–3 minutes on each side for medium-rare, or until cooked to your liking. Rest for 3 minutes before slicing very thinly, and serve with chicken or beef gravy instead.

HEALTHY FATS
HIGH IN PROTEIN

- Almost 1½ serves protein per serve
- Great source of vitamin B₁₂
- Good source of potassium + vitamin A

MAKE AHEAD
You can make the braised lamb, stock and gravy all in advance. Freeze in separate airtight containers for up to 3 months.

DINNER TIME

DAIRY FREEABLE • NUT FREE • EGG FREE

CHICKEN AND VEG PIE 'TIL YOU DIE Serves 4

A traditional chicken and vegetable pie, topped with flaky, buttery pastry, is a real comfort food, but this reworking of the humble classic really ticks all the boxes, with its tasty gravy and filo pastry topping — while serving up only half the calories and saturated fat, and just a quarter of the carbs. My husband loves to offer suggestions when I experiment with new dishes, but even I was taken aback when he suggested this pie had too much chicken (at only 250 g/9 oz). Whatever quantity of chicken you choose, this pie will certainly fill you up. For a dairy-free version, omit the butter.

3
SERVES VEG
per serve

1 tablespoon olive oil, plus extra
   for drizzling
2 tablespoons plain flour
250–400 g (9–14 oz) boneless, skinless
   free-range chicken thighs, trimmed,
   cut into 3 cm (1¼ inch) chunks
1 teaspoon fennel or coriander seeds
   (see tips)
1 tablespoon butter (optional)
1 large leek, white part only, thinly
   sliced (see tips)
2 carrots, scrubbed and cut into 1.5 cm
   (¾ inch) pieces
1 small celeriac (or 1 large parsnip and
   1 celery stalk), peeled and cut into
   1.5 cm (¾ inch) pieces
1 tablespoon dijon mustard
1 tablespoon finely chopped tarragon
   or sage, or 1 teaspoon finely chopped
   rosemary
½ quantity (300 ml) Chicken gravy
   (page 221)
6–8 asparagus spears, woody stems
   removed, cut into 2 cm (¾ inch)
   lengths
10 sheets filo pastry

Preheat the oven to 180°C (350°F).

Heat the oil in a large frying pan over medium–high heat. Put the flour in a bowl, season with sea salt and freshly ground black pepper, add the chicken and toss until well coated. Add the chicken to the pan and cook for 2 minutes, or until lightly browned, turning regularly. Remove to a bowl and set aside.

Reduce the heat to medium. Toast the fennel seeds in the pan for 20 seconds, or until fragrant. Add the butter, if using, and the leek. Cook for 2 minutes, then transfer to the bowl with the chicken.

Heat another 2 teaspoons oil in the pan over medium heat. Add the carrot and celeriac and cook, stirring, for 8–10 minutes, until just tender. Stir in the mustard, herbs and gravy until combined.

Return the chicken mixture and juices to the pan. Bring to a simmer, then transfer to an 8 cup (2 litre) pie dish. Stir the asparagus through and set aside.

Lay out half the filo sheets on a clean work surface. Drizzle or spray each sheet with oil, then scrunch up and place on top of the pie filling. Repeat with the remaining pastry sheets. When finished, drizzle or spray the top with more oil.

Bake for 30 minutes, or until the pastry is golden. Serve warm.

TOP TIPS
- Try using 400 g (14 oz) sweet potato instead of the celeriac, and broccolini instead of asparagus.
- Fennel seeds add a wonderful flavour to a chicken pie, and also aid digestion. I like to use a combination of both fennel and coriander seeds. It's a great way to introduce different spices to young family members.
- I like to use as much of the leek as possible, including some of the greener bit of the stalk, before it starts branching out at the top. You'll need to thoroughly rinse between all the layers to remove any grit, and the greener bits will take a little longer to tenderise, but recipes like this and the fish pie opposite are the perfect way to make use of them.

(see photo page 125)

HEALTHY FATS
HIGH IN PROTEIN
LOWER CARB

- 1½ serves protein per serve
- Great source of fibre and selenium

MAKE AHEAD
Make a double batch of the filling and freeze half in an airtight container for up to 3 months.

TRY MY FISH PIE Serves 4

Fish pie is such a British classic, but is normally laden with dairy and saturated fat. Not this version, which cleverly uses a plant-based white sauce. I find that hiding all the healthy vegies inside the pie, rather than just serving them on the side, creates a bit more fun and mystery. Vegies galore in this one!

6½
SERVES VEG
per serve

800 g (1 lb 12 oz) root vegetables, such as celeriac, sweet potato, parsnip and/or potato, scrubbed or peeled, then cut into 1.5 cm (⅝ inch) pieces

1 tablespoon olive oil, plus extra for drizzling

1–2 leeks, white part only, halved lengthways and thinly sliced (see tip on opposite page)

2 cups (500 ml) White sauce (page 193)

splash of milk (optional)

400 g (14 oz) skinless, boneless salmon or firm white fish (or a combination), cut into 3 cm (1¼ inch) cubes

1 tablespoon finely chopped dill, tarragon or thyme

200 g (7 oz) snow peas (mangetout) or sugar snap peas, halved

Preheat the oven to 220°C (425°F). Put the root vegetables on a baking tray, drizzle with oil and season with sea salt and freshly ground black pepper, tossing to coat. Spread out in a single layer and bake for 15–20 minutes, or until tender.

Meanwhile, heat the oil in a large deep frying pan over medium–high heat. Add the leek and sauté for 3–5 minutes, or until lightly golden. Season with salt and pepper. Stir in the white sauce until combined, adding a little milk or water if you'd like a thinner consistency. Warm through for 1–2 minutes, then stir in the fish, herbs and snow peas. Transfer to a 6–8 cup (1.5–2 litre) pie dish.

When the vegetables have finished baking, roughly mash them on the baking tray, then spread them over the pie filling as a topping.

Bake for 5–10 minutes, or until the topping is golden and the fish is cooked through. Serve immediately.

TOP TIPS

- The white sauce will thicken during cooking, so if you like a fish pie with a lot of sauce, add about ½ cup (125 ml) milk of your choice.
- For a vegan or dairy-free white sauce, omit the cheese and use olive oil instead of butter. Thin the white sauce with a plant-based milk if needed.

DIVIDE AND CONQUER

- Make little fish-free vegan pies in individual heatproof dishes, using the same white sauce and vegetable mixture. Instead of the fish you could add small broccoli florets and/or tinned cannellini beans, or add extra protein by scattering over some toasted slivered almonds, pepitas (pumpkin seeds) or sunflower seeds.

(see photo page 125)

HEALTHY FATS
HIGH IN PROTEIN

- 1 serve protein per serve
- 50% RDI fibre + 40% RDI selenium + 25% RDI calcium per serve (from the fish)
- Great source of vitamins B_{12} + C
- Good source of iron (from fish, tofu, snow peas)

STEAK AND KIDNEY BEAN PIE Serves 4

I'm not a huge fan of kidneys, even though they're very nutritious, being extremely high in vitamin B_2 and B_{12} — but kidney beans are good for you too, with 1 cup yielding twice as much iron as 90 g (3 oz) beef. They make a great substitute for kidneys in this meaty pie, contributing a satisfying flavour and texture that pairs deliciously well with beef. This version is lower in calories and much higher in fibre than a standard steak and kidney pie. A winner on all counts.

just under 4 SERVES VEG per serve

2 tablespoons olive oil

1 large red onion, finely chopped

2 garlic cloves, crushed or finely chopped

3 carrots, scrubbed or peeled, quartered and thinly sliced

400 g (14 oz) mushrooms, chopped

1 tablespoon fresh thyme leaves

2½ tablespoons tomato paste (concentrated purée)

½ quantity Beef gravy (page 225)

1 tablespoon worcestershire sauce

400 g (14 oz) tin kidney beans, drained well

1 quantity braised beef, from the Beef stock recipe on page 224, or 250–400 g (9–14 oz) lean minced beef

1 quantity My shortcrust pastry (page 204)

Preheat the oven to 180°C (350°F).

Heat 1 tablespoon of the oil in a large deep frying pan over medium–high heat. Cook the onion, garlic and carrot for 5 minutes, stirring often, then transfer to a greased 6–8 cup (1.5–2 litre) pie dish.

Heat the remaining oil in the pan. Add the mushrooms and thyme and cook, stirring, for 5 minutes. Return the sautéed vegetables to the pan, stir in the tomato paste and cook for a further 1 minute.

Stir in the gravy, worcestershire sauce, kidney beans and beef and cook for 2 minutes, or until the liquid has thickened slightly. Transfer the mixture to the pie dish.

On a clean work surface, roll out the pastry so it is 2.5 cm (1 inch) larger than the diameter of the top of the pie dish. From all the way around the outside edge of the pastry round, cut off a 5 mm (¼ inch) strip; it doesn't have to be in one long piece. Set aside.

Lightly brush the rim of the pie dish with water, then press the pastry strips onto the rim to cover it; this 'collar' will help stop the pastry lid sliding off the pie during baking.

Lightly brush the pastry rim with water, then place the pastry lid over the pie, pressing on the edges to seal. Trim away any excess pastry, then crimp the edges together with the back of a fork to seal. Make a cross incision in the centre of the pie lid with the tip of a sharp knife.

Bake for 35–40 minutes, or until the pastry is golden and cooked. Remove from the oven and leave to stand for 5–10 minutes before serving.

TOP TIPS

- It is quickest and easiest to use a food processor to chop or slice the onion, carrots and mushrooms.
- For a dairy-free pie, use olive oil instead of butter in the gravy.

HIGH IN PROTEIN

+
- 1½ serves protein per serve
- Almost 1½ serves legumes per serve
- Great source of fibre + vitamin B_{12}

MAKE AHEAD
Make a double batch of the filling and freeze half in an airtight container for up to 3 months.

CHICKEN AND VEG PIE 'TIL YOU DIE
(see recipe page 122)

TRY MY FISH PIE
(see recipe page 123)

STEAK AND KIDNEY BEAN PIE

DREAMY NOT-SO-CREAMY CHICKEN PASTA Serves 4

2¹/2 SERVES VEG per serve

This was my go-to dish as a kid when we used to visit our local Italian restaurant. I couldn't get enough of it — but then again I never really understood what I was eating. Funnily enough, this version is so convincing I felt guilty eating it the first time I made it. Minus the chives, it's the perfect 'white diet' food that even young children will love.

300 g (10½ oz) long pasta of your choice, such as linguine

2 tablespoons olive oil

250 g (9 oz) boneless, skinless free-range chicken breast or tenderloins, cut into 1.5 cm (⅝ inch) pieces

500 g (1 lb 2 oz) mushrooms, such as Swiss browns, cleaned and thinly sliced

3 cups (750 ml) White sauce (page 193)

1 teaspoon dried oregano or mixed Italian herbs

2 tablespoons finely chopped chives (optional)

Bring a large saucepan of salted water to the boil. Add the pasta and cook according to the packet instructions.

Meanwhile, heat 1 tablespoon of the oil in a large frying pan over high heat. Season the chicken with salt and freshly ground black pepper and cook for 3 minutes, or until golden. Remove the chicken to a bowl and keep warm.

Add the remaining oil to the pan and cook the mushrooms for 5 minutes, or until golden, tossing the pan constantly. Season with salt and pepper and reduce the heat to medium–low.

Once the pasta is cooked, immediately remove the pasta from the boiling water with tongs and drop it straight into the pan of mushrooms. Add the white sauce and herbs, return the chicken to the pan and cook for 2 minutes, or until heated through.

Serve sprinkled with the chives, if desired.

TOP TIPS
- For a dairy-free meal, use olive oil and omit the cheese when making the white sauce.
- For gluten free, use a gluten-free pasta.

DIVIDE AND CONQUER
- You can increase the mushrooms for vegans, and add different ones to mix it up; use olive oil and omit the cheese when making the white sauce. Cook and serve the chicken separately.

HEALTHY FATS HIGH IN PROTEIN

- 1 serve protein per serve
- 50% RDI fibre per serve
- No added sugars

FINGER-LICKIN' FISH FINGERS Serves 4

9 SERVES VEG per serve

Growing up, I'm not sure I ever liked fish fingers very much — unlike many of the other 'unhealthier' foods I used to enjoy as a kid. My daughter definitely likes these ones, though, as they're pretty special, being made from fresh salmon. Instead of flour and eggs, I like to use white sauce as a base for the crumbs to stick to. It really adds to the recipe, not just in terms of bumping up the veg intake, but especially the flavour. I've turned these fish fingers into more of a meal by adding chips and mushy peas, though you could also serve the fish fingers with Creamed corn (page 213) and Roasted potato mash (page 218).

750 g (1 lb 10 oz) parsnips or sweet potato (or a combination), scrubbed or peeled, cut into chips

neutral-flavoured oil, such as rice bran or grapeseed oil, for shallow-frying and drizzling

1 quantity warm Mushy peas (see tip on page 213)

2 cups (120 g) fresh spelt or gluten-free breadcrumbs

¾ cup (185 ml) White sauce (page 193); optional (see tip)

400 g (14 oz) skinless, boneless salmon, cut into 12 evenly sized 'fingers'

Preheat the oven to 200°C (400°F). Line two baking trays with baking paper.

Spread the vegetable chips on one baking tray, drizzle with oil and season with sea salt. Roast for 15–20 minutes, or until tender.

Meanwhile, warm the mushy peas in a saucepan and keep warm over low heat.

Pour enough oil into a large frying pan to come 1.5 cm (⅝ inch) up the side. Heat the oil to 180°C (350°F), or until a cube of bread dropped into the oil turns golden brown in 15 seconds.

Meanwhile, place the breadcrumbs in a wide shallow bowl, and the white sauce in another bowl. Coat the salmon pieces in the white sauce, then coat them well in the breadcrumbs.

In batches, cook the fish fingers for 1–2 minutes on each side, or until golden and cooked through. Drain well on paper towel, season with salt and keep warm in the oven on the second baking tray while cooking the remainder.

Serve the fish fingers immediately, with the hot chips and mushy peas.

TOP TIPS

- If you don't have any white sauce made up, simply dust the fish fingers in seasoned wholemeal plain flour, shaking off the excess. In a shallow bowl, lightly beat 2 eggs, then dip the fish fingers in the egg to coat, then coat them with the breadcrumbs.
- For a dairy-free meal, use olive oil instead of butter in the mushy peas and white sauce. When making the white sauce, also omit the cheese.
- For gluten-free fish fingers, use gluten-free breadcrumbs.

HEALTHY FATS
HIGH IN PROTEIN

- 1 serve protein per serve
- 75% RDI phosphorus (mostly from fish, then peas)
+ 20% RDI calcium (mostly from parsnips) per serve
- Great source of fibre
- Good source of iron and zinc (from mushy peas)

MAKE AHEAD
The uncooked, coated fish fingers freeze well for up to 3 months; just be sure to use fresh (not frozen) fish. Freeze in a single layer on baking paper, with space in between; once frozen, you can stack them in an airtight container. Thaw in the fridge before cooking.

CALL-IT-TUNA MAC 'N' CHEESE Serves 4–6

When it comes to tinned fish, I feel better about giving my daughter sardines or mackerel rather than tuna. Try calling it 'tuna' and using mackerel or sardines here instead: you may well be surprised! My daughter fully accepts that this is what mac 'n' cheese is and she loves it. Sardines may seem a bit of a stretch, but these days there are some really good-quality ones available. You can of course use tinned tuna here, or keep it totally vegetarian if you prefer.

**3
SERVES VEG
per serve**

2 cups (300 g) gluten-free macaroni, such as brown rice macaroni

3 cups (750 ml) White sauce (page 193)

½ cup (125 ml) milk or non-dairy milk

½ cup (50 g) finely grated parmesan, pecorino or provolone cheese

⅔ cup (100 g) mixed nuts and seeds, such as almonds, pistachios, pepitas (pumpkin seeds), sunflower or sesame seeds (see tip)

250 g (9 oz) tin wild-caught mackerel or sardines, drained and flaked

1 cup (220 g) coarsely chopped artichokes, marinated or in brine

1⅓ cups (200 g) frozen peas or corn (or a combination), thawed

green salad, to serve

Preheat the oven to 200°C (400°F).

Bring a saucepan of salted water to the boil and cook the macaroni for about three-quarters of the time recommended on the packet instructions.

Meanwhile, in a large saucepan, warm the white sauce and milk over low heat. Combine the cheese, mixed nuts and seeds in a bowl.

Drain the macaroni and add to the white sauce, along with the fish, artichokes and frozen vegetables, stirring well to combine.

Transfer the mixture to a 10 cup (2.5 litre) baking dish. Sprinkle with the nut and seed mixture. Bake on the middle shelf of the oven for 10 minutes, or until the pasta is al dente and the topping is golden.

Remove and set aside to rest for 5 minutes, before serving with a green salad.

TOP TIPS

• Any of your favourite nuts and seeds will make a nutritious, crunchy topping for this dish. If someone in the family has a nut allergy, mix some breadcrumbs (gluten-free or spelt) with the cheese instead.

DIVIDE AND CONQUER

• For vegans, use cauliflower florets instead of fish. When making the white sauce, use olive oil instead of butter and omit the cheese, leaving it out of the macaroni bake as well. Use non-dairy milk in the macaroni mixture. Divide the macaroni mixture among individual ceramic heatproof bowls and bake the two different versions separately.

**HEALTHY FATS
HIGH IN PROTEIN**

• 3 serves wholegrains per serve
• Almost 1½ serves protein per serve
• Great source of folate and vitamin B_{12}

UPSIDE-DOWN CHICKEN KIEV Serves 4

Here we're turning chicken kiev on its head. Instead of stuffing a chicken breast with garlic butter, we're stuffing a garlic-butter-chicken stuffing into baked sweet potato jackets! I must admit I've never actually eaten a homemade chicken kiev. Very occasionally, when mum was too tired or time-strapped to cook, she'd heat up the frozen kind for the family dinner. I do have fond memories of them, but look at the packet and you'll see they're full of unidentifiable ingredients! Well, not these ones.

9
SERVES VEG
per serve

4 × 300–400 g (10½–14 oz) sweet
  potatoes, scrubbed well
1 tablespoon extra virgin olive oil,
  plus extra for drizzling
400–500 g (1 lb–1 lb 2 oz) kale, stems
  discarded, leaves torn into 6–8 cm
  (2½–3 inch) pieces
½ cup (75 g) sunflower seeds, pepitas
  (pumpkin seeds) and/or chopped
  or slivered almonds
1½ tablespoons butter
2 garlic cloves, finely chopped
  or crushed
1 tablespoon finely chopped parsley
  (optional)
1 red capsicum (pepper), cut into 1 cm
  (½ inch) pieces
½ quantity Chicken stuffing (page 219),
  warmed

Preheat the oven to 200°C (400°F). Line two large baking trays with baking paper.

Prick the sweet potatoes all over with a fork, drizzle with oil, season all over with sea salt and place on one of the baking trays. Roast for 50 minutes, or until a skewer can be inserted easily.

Meanwhile, massage the kale with oil and lightly season with salt, being careful not to add too much, as kale is naturally salty. Arrange in a single layer on the other baking tray and bake on a lower shelf of the oven for the last 10 minutes of the sweet potato cooking time. Toast the seeds and nuts in the oven for the last 5 minutes.

While the vegetables are in the oven, melt the butter in a small saucepan over medium heat. Add the garlic and stir for 30 seconds, or until lightly golden. Turn off the heat and stir in the parsley, if using. Set aside.

Meanwhile, heat the 1 tablespoon oil over medium heat. Fry the capsicum for 3–5 minutes, or until softened, then add the chicken stuffing and mix until well combined and the stuffing is warm. Set aside.

When the sweet potatoes are ready, remove them from the oven. While they are still piping hot, carefully use a sharp knife to make a lengthways incision along the top of each sweet potato, through the middle, taking care not to cut all the way through. Use a fork to fluff up the centre.

Drizzle the sweet potatoes with the garlic butter, top with the chicken mixture and sprinkle with the nuts and seeds. Serve immediately, with the kale chips.

TOP TIPS
• If you don't have chicken stuffing, use some shredded barbecued chicken.
• You can swap the capsicum for 200 g (7 oz) wilted English spinach leaves.

DIVIDE AND CONQUER
• To make half the dish vegan, use olive oil instead of butter. Use only half the quantity of chicken, keeping it separate for the omnivores. For the vegans, sauté 500 g (1 lb 2 oz) mushrooms, and add some wilted English spinach leaves.

HEALTHY FATS
HIGH IN PROTEIN

• Almost 1½ serves protein per serve
• 400% RDI vitamins A + C per serve
• 20% RDI of calcium (from potatoes, kale, capsicum)
• Good source of iron (potatoes, seeds, kale, herbs)

QUICK 'ROAST' PORK DINNER WITH 'CRACKLING', APPLE SAUCE AND GRAVY Serves 4

We all love a good roast, but they're often time consuming, expensive and intimidating to prepare. Well, not this one. This is your roast dinner reinvented, and epitomises the whole 'three veg and one meat' philosophy. Each serve is high in protein and fibre, contains healthy fats, *and* achieves your daily vegetable quota, without losing any of the flavour that you would expect from a roast dinner. Plus you can still enjoy the 'crackling', by serving the rice crackers on top of the pork. Gets me every time.

**5 1/2
SERVES VEG
per serve**

800 g (1 lb 12 oz) pumpkin, seeds removed, peeled if desired, then cut into 5 cm (2 inch) chunks

1 leek, white part only, thinly sliced

2 green apples, unpeeled, cut into quarters, core removed

2 garlic cloves, unpeeled

1 tablespoon olive oil, plus extra for drizzling

2 small heads of broccoli, quartered

300–350 g (10½–12 oz) piece of pork fillet (see tips), sinew removed

1 tablespoon white wine vinegar or cider vinegar

1½ tablespoons maple syrup, or 2 teaspoons sugar

4 tablespoons coarsely chopped mint

½ teaspoon toasted fennel seeds (optional)

4 cups (200 g) baby English spinach leaves, washed well

Scratch, cracklin' pop (page 199), to serve (optional)

hot Mushroom gravy (page 217) or Chicken gravy (page 221), to serve (optional)

Preheat the oven to 200°C (400°F) fan-forced. Line a large baking tray with baking paper. Arrange the pumpkin on one half of the baking tray. On the other side, arrange the leek, apples and garlic cloves. Drizzle the ingredients with oil and season with sea salt and freshly ground black pepper, tossing to coat.

Roast for 10 minutes, then remove the apples, leek and garlic from the tray and set aside. Return the pumpkin to the oven for another 5 minutes, then add the broccoli to the tray, drizzle with oil, season with salt and bake for a final 10 minutes, or until the vegetables are tender.

Meanwhile, in a large frying pan, heat the oil over high heat. Season the pork on all sides with salt and pepper. Cook for 8–10 minutes, turning occasionally, until golden and just cooked through. Set aside to rest in a warm place, reserving the pan.

When the garlic cloves are cool enough to handle, squeeze the flesh from the skins into a small saucepan. Add the roasted leek and apple, vinegar, maple syrup, mint and 1 cup (250 ml) water. Using a stick blender, process to a purée. Season to taste and stir in the toasted fennel seeds, if using. Keep warm over low heat.

Meanwhile, reheat the frying pan over high heat. Cook the spinach for 2 minutes, or until wilted, stirring often. Season to taste.

Just before serving, cut the pork into 1 cm (½ inch) thick slices. Serve immediately, with the roasted vegetables, spinach and apple sauce, and the 'crackling' and gravy if desired.

TOP TIPS

- This recipe works well with 4 × 75 g (2½ oz) pork loin steaks. Heat 1 tablespoon oil in a frying pan over high heat. Season the steaks with salt and pepper and cook for 2 minutes each side, or until just cooked through.
- For dairy free, use olive oil in the gravy. For gluten free, use gluten-free flour and cornflour in the gravy, and gluten-free soy sauce in the crackers.

**HEALTHY FATS
HIGH IN PROTEIN**

- Over 1 serve protein per serve
- 250% RDI vitamin C per serve
- Great source of fibre (from vegetables)
- Good source of iron (from spinach, broccoli, pumpkin, then pork)

MAKE AHEAD

The apple sauce makes about 2 cups (500 ml), so you can freeze any leftovers in an airtight container for your next roast.

MEGA MEATBALL SUBS Serves 4

Big on flavour, these meaty-looking, dude-food subs feel pretty indulgent, and are oh so satisfying. Watch the whole family gobble up a healthy amount of veg without a second thought! The vego balls are by far my favourite in these subs, but you can easily mix it up if anyone isn't a mushroom fan, or is nut free.

2 SERVES VEG per serve

4 sub rolls

2 tablespoons olive oil

16 uncooked meatballs of your choice, preferably Beef, lamb, or veal and pork meatballs (page 232), or Vego balls (page 227)

400 ml (14 fl oz) Roasted tomato passata (page 207), or store-bought tomato passata (puréed tomatoes)

½ teaspoon chilli flakes (optional)

⅔ cup (80 g) coarsely grated cheese, such as provolone, fontina or mozzarella

rocket (arugula) leaves, to serve

pickled jalapeño chillies, to serve (optional)

Preheat the oven to 170°C (325°F).

Make an incision in the rolls, lengthways down the middle, along the top — taking care not to cut all the way through. Wrap each roll individually in foil. Warm in the oven for 10 minutes, or until heated through.

Meanwhile, heat the oil in a large frying pan over medium heat. Cook the meatballs for 5 minutes, or until golden. (If cooking the vego balls, take care as the mixture is softer than a typical meatball mixture.) Carefully turn them over using a spoon.

Reduce the heat to low and add the passata and chilli, if using. Cook for a further 5 minutes, or until the sauce has thickened and the meatballs are cooked through. For a thinner sauce consistency, if needed, stir in up to 3 tablespoons water until combined.

Divide the meatballs among the warm rolls and top with the cheese, rocket and jalapeño chilli, if using. Serve immediately.

TOP TIPS

- It's so handy to have a batch or two of different meatball mixtures prepared ahead and stashed away in the freezer, for quick meals like this.
- For vegan subs, use vego balls and omit the cheese.
- For nut-free subs, use beef or lamb meatballs, rather than vego balls.

HEALTHY FATS HIGH IN PROTEIN

- 1½ serves protein per serve
- 1 serve legumes per serve
- Great source of fibre
- Good source of calcium

**MIDDLE-EASTERN
NACHOS**

(see recipe page 140)

ASIAN NACHOS
(see recipe page 141)

MIDDLE-EASTERN NACHOS Serves 4

Just about everyone loves nachos, a humble Mexican dish popular the world over. Here's a cross-cultural reimagining of an old classic: a quick, colourful and exotically spiced version, starring lamb and eggplant, and topped with pomegranate seeds.

just under
1½
SERVES VEG
per serve

1 small eggplant (aubergine), cut into 1 cm (½ inch) chunks

extra virgin olive oil, for drizzling or spraying

3 wholemeal Lebanese breads, cut into wedges

250–400 g (9–14 oz) minced lamb or chicken

3 tablespoons pine nuts

3 teaspoons za'atar or baharat (or 1½ teaspoons each ground coriander and cumin)

1 garlic clove, crushed or finely chopped (optional)

400 g (14 oz) tin lentils, borlotti beans or chickpeas (or any pulses you like)

200 g (7 oz) cherry tomatoes, halved or quartered

1 Lebanese cucumber

½ cup (135 g) Sour-ish cream (page 192)

1 tablespoon tahini

seeds from 1 pomegranate (optional)

Line two baking trays with baking paper. Place the eggplant on one baking tray, drizzle with oil and season with sea salt. Toss to coat, then spread the eggplant out in a single layer. Put the tray in the oven and set the oven to 180°C (350°F).

On the second baking tray, arrange the bread wedges in a single layer. Drizzle or spray the bread with oil on both sides and lightly season with sea salt. Once the oven comes up to temperature, remove the eggplant and add the bread. Bake the bread for 8 minutes, or until golden and crisp, keeping an eye on it.

Meanwhile, put the lamb, eggplant, pine nuts and za'atar in a large frying pan. Season with salt, add the garlic, if using, and place over medium heat. Cook, stirring, for 6–8 minutes, or until the fat starts to render from the meat and the lamb is browned. Add the lentils and tomatoes and cook, stirring, for a further 5 minutes, or until the tomatoes have softened slightly.

Halve the cucumber lengthways. Scoop the seeds into a small bowl, stir in the sour-ish cream and tahini and season to taste with a pinch of salt. Cut the cucumber flesh into small chunks and place in another small bowl. Lightly season with salt and combine with the pomegranate seeds, if using.

Serve the lamb mixture with the crispy bread wedges, tahini cream and cucumber salsa.

TOP TIPS

- Lamb can be quite fatty, so you won't need to add any extra oil to the frying pan. It's good to start cooking it in a cold frying pan, to allow the fat to be released slowly (a process known as rendering).
- Garnish the dish with chopped spring onion (scallion), parsley and/or mint.
- Omit the sour-ish cream to make the dish dairy free.

DIVIDE AND CONQUER

- For vegans, use a 400 g (14 oz) tin of lentils instead of the lamb; replace the sour-ish cream with the Lemon tahini dressing on page 58.
- You could cook some lamb separately and stir it through half the topping mixture just before serving, for those who would like a meat version.

(see photo page 138)

HEALTHY FATS
HIGH IN PROTEIN

+

- 1½ serves protein per serve
- 1 serve legumes per serve
- Good source of fibre

ASIAN NACHOS Serves 4

Here's another fresh twist on an old favourite. Corn chips make way for wonton crisps, pork puts in an appearance, water chestnuts add crunch and texture, and the whole beany mix takes on distinctly Asian flavours. If you have some Sesame salt (page 200) on hand, or even peanuts, you can sprinkle a little over just before serving for added texture.

3 SERVES VEG per serve

270 g (9½ oz) packet of square wonton wrappers

2 teaspoons neutral-flavoured oil, such as grapeseed, plus extra for brushing or spraying

250 g (9 oz) minced pork

5 tablespoons oyster sauce

1 avocado

juice of ½ lime

2 spring onions (scallions), thinly sliced, or a small handful of coarsely chopped coriander (cilantro)

3 teaspoons cornflour

1 teaspoon raw sugar

1 tablespoon sesame oil

1 tablespoon finely grated fresh ginger

1 carrot, coarsely grated (optional)

400 g (14 oz) tin black beans, drained, or 200 g (7 oz) frozen peeled edamame beans (or a combination)

225 g (8 oz) tin chopped water chestnuts, drained

sriracha sauce, to serve (optional)

Preheat the oven to 180°C (350°F). Line a large baking tray with baking paper.

Cut the wonton wrappers in half, into triangles. Spread them out on the baking tray and lightly brush or spray on both sides with oil. Bake for 6 minutes, or until golden and crisp. Remove from the oven so they don't burn, but stay crisp.

Meanwhile, combine the pork with 2 tablespoons of the oyster sauce in a bowl. Set aside briefly for the flavour to infuse the pork.

Scoop the avocado flesh into a bowl. Add the lime juice and mash with a fork. Season to taste with sea salt, stir in about 1 tablespoon of the spring onion and set aside.

In a bowl, mix together the cornflour and 150 ml (5 fl oz) water. Whisk in the sugar and the remaining 3 tablespoons oyster sauce until smooth.

Heat the 2 teaspoons of oil in a wok or large deep frying pan over medium heat. Stir-fry the pork mixture for 5 minutes, then remove to a bowl.

Add the sesame oil, ginger and carrot to the wok. Once it starts sizzling, stir-fry for 1 minute.

Give the cornflour mixture another quick stir to bring it back together, then add to the wok and cook for a further minute. If using the black beans, add them now, break them down a bit with a wooden spoon and cook for a further minute.

Return the pork to the wok with the water chestnuts, and the edamame beans, if using. Stir well to combine, then cook for a further minute, or until heated through.

Serve the pork mixture with the wonton crisps, guacamole, remaining spring onion and a drizzle of sriracha sauce if desired.

DIVIDE AND CONQUER

- For vegans, use 300 g (10½ oz) silken tofu instead of minced pork (or cook some pork separately to stir through at the end for those who would like it). Add the tofu at the same time as the beans; it will break up as it is soft, but will taste delicious. Also use a vegetarian oyster sauce, which you'll sometimes find called 'vegetarian stir-fry sauce'.

(see photo page 139)

**HEALTHY FATS
HIGH IN PROTEIN**

- 1½ serves protein + 1 serve legumes per serve
- High in fibre
- Good source of calcium (from edamame beans)
- Good source of folate (from avocado)

DEEP-DISH PIZZA Serves 4–6

I'll never forget dining at the original deep-dish pizza restaurant in Chicago, biting into one of the richest, most disgustingly delicious dishes of my life — the ultimate indulgence. Well, your family won't forget this pizza either. It takes a little work, but it's definitely a special treat, containing just enough melty cheese to convince the kids it's full of the stuff, vegetables that could pass as pepperoni, a pizza dough that is full of protein and calcium-packed chickpeas — the list goes on. What pizza, especially a deep-dish one, is low in cholesterol? This one is! To list a few comparisons, one serve of a traditional deep-dish pizza typically has two and a half times as much saturated fat, double the carbs and a third of the fibre of this version. This one has only about two-thirds of the calories, too — so you needn't feel quite so guilty about digging in.

2¹/₂ SERVES VEG per serve

3 tablespoons olive oil

1 teaspoon coarse polenta or cornmeal (optional)

1 quantity Pizza dough (page 205)

110 g (4 oz) ball of buffalo mozzarella, thinly sliced, or ¾ cup (65 g) melty cheese such as fontina

½ cup (50 g) roasted capsicum (pepper) strips

¼ cup (40 g) pitted kalamata or green olives

2 teaspoons capers, drained

4 anchovies (optional)

1 quantity Pepperini (page 209)

1 quantity Pizza sauce (page 206)

¼ cup (20 g) finely grated parmesan cheese (optional)

Preheat the oven to 220°C (425°F).

Put the olive oil in a cast-iron pan or heavy-based ovenproof frying pan measuring 20 cm (8 inches) across the base, 25 cm (10 inches) across the top, and 5 cm (2 inches) deep. Brush to coat the base and sides of the pan with oil. Evenly sprinkle with the polenta, if using.

Roll the dough out to about 5 mm (¼ inch) thick, then carefully and evenly press it into the pan. Cover the dough base with the cheese slices. Scatter with the capsicum strips, olives, capers and anchovies, if using. Cover the surface with the pepperini, then evenly spread the pizza sauce over. Sprinkle with the parmesan, if using.

Place the pan over medium heat for 5 minutes, then transfer to the oven and bake for a further 15–20 minutes, or until the dough is golden and cooked.

Remove from the oven and stand for 5–10 minutes before slicing.

This pizza can be deliciously messy to eat, so keep some wet hand towels on hand when serving.

TOP TIP
- A heavy-based cast-iron pan is typically used for this dish, which you can buy inexpensively and 'season' at home. Alternatively, you could use a cake tin, pressing the dough 5 cm (2 inches) up the sides.

DIVIDE AND CONQUER
- You can easily make the pizza vegetarian on one side, sprinkling with a little extra cheese to distinguish it. If you don't want to use cheese, use 1–2 cups (250–500 ml) White sauce (page 193) instead.

**HEALTHY FATS
LOW CHOLESTEROL
(20 MG PER SERVE)**

- 2 serves wholegrains per serve
- 1 serve legumes + ½ serve protein per serve
- Great source of fibre and vitamin C
- Good source of iron (mostly from chickpeas)

THREE-VEG MEDLEY WITH FISH Serves 4

3 SERVES VEG per serve

This fabulous dish is such a super simple and satisfying way to introduce the family to the idea of 'three veg and meat'. Too easy.

3 tablespoons extra virgin olive oil

400 g (14 oz) boneless firm white fish fillet, such as barramundi or snapper, with or without skin

3 zucchini (courgettes), cut into 5 cm (2 inch) batons

1 large roasted capsicum (pepper), cut into 4 cm (1½ inch) strips

½ cup (75 g) pine nuts or slivered almonds

1 garlic clove, finely chopped or crushed

1–2 tablespoons finely chopped parsley

1 quantity Creamed corn (page 213), warmed

Heat 1 tablespoon of the oil in a large frying pan over medium–high heat. Season the fish with sea salt and freshly ground black pepper. Add the fish to one side of the pan, placing it skin side down if it has skin on. Cook for 3–4 minutes, or until golden underneath.

Turn the fish over, then add the zucchini to the other side of the pan. Cook for 2–3 minutes, depending on the thickness of the fish, until the fish is cooked through, sautéing the zucchini until golden and tender, and stirring in the capsicum for the last minute to warm through.

Meanwhile, put the remaining 2 tablespoons oil in a small saucepan with the pine nuts and garlic over medium–low heat. Cook, stirring, for about 3 minutes, or until the nuts and garlic are lightly golden. Stir in the parsley, season with salt and pepper and remove from the heat.

Divide the creamed corn and vegetables among four serving plates. Flake the fish over, drizzle with the pine nut mixture and serve.

TOP TIPS

- If you can't find one whole 400 g (14 oz) piece of fish, you can use several smaller pieces, and slightly reduce the cooking time.
- For a dairy-free meal, use olive oil rather than butter in the creamed corn.

**HEALTHY FATS
HIGH IN PROTEIN
LOW CARB**

- 1½ serves protein per serve
- 80% RDI vitamin B_{12} per serve
- Great source of vitamins C and E

AMEN FOR MY RAMEN Serves 4

Tonkotsu ramen is well known for its very long simmering of pork bones, breaking down the collagen, marrow and fat, turning the stock creamy, rich and white. This version contains quite a few ingredients that give you that pop of 'umami' savouriness: mushrooms, kombu dashi, mushrooms, miso paste, soy sauce, tomatoes. It has only half the calories of a traditional tonkotsu ramen, is low in saturated fat, and is ready in a fraction of the time. For a vegan ramen, omit the boiled eggs.

**2
SERVES VEG
per serve**

4 × 4 g (⅛ oz) sachets of kombu dashi
  powder
4 large dried shiitake mushrooms
1 tablespoon grapeseed oil, rice bran
  oil, or even light olive oil
2 onions, coarsely chopped
1 carrot, coarsely chopped
4 garlic cloves, coarsely chopped
4 cm (1½ inch) piece of fresh ginger,
  peeled and thinly sliced
120 g (4 oz) white miso paste
  (about 5 tablespoons)
90 ml (3 fl oz) mirin
4 roma tomatoes, halved lengthways
4 tablespoons Chinese sesame paste
  or tahini (see tips on page 194)
1 tablespoon rice vinegar
2 tablespoons cooking sake
4 tablespoons soy sauce
300 g (10½ oz) dried ramen noodles,
  or 500 g (1 lb 2 oz) fresh noodles

To serve
2 soft-boiled eggs (see tip, page 54),
  shelled and cut in half
1 nori sheet, cut into 4 squares,
  or seaweed snacks
Sesame salt (page 200)
thinly sliced spring onion (scallion)

Put the kombu dashi and dried mushrooms in a large heatproof jug. Add 4 cups (1 litre) boiling water, stirring to dissolve the dashi powder. Cover and set aside for at least 30 minutes to soften the mushrooms, then discard the woody stems.

Heat the oil in a large saucepan over high heat. Add the onion, carrot, garlic and ginger and cook, stirring constantly, for 3–5 minutes, or until the onion is charred and deep golden. Reduce the heat to medium and add the kombu stock and mushrooms, adding 6 cups (1.5 litres) water to make up 10 cups (2.5 litres). Bring the broth to just below a simmer, then reduce the heat to low and cook for 45 minutes to allow the flavours to develop.

Meanwhile, preheat the oven to 180°C (350°F). Line a small baking tray with baking paper. Combine 1 tablespoon of the miso paste and 2 teaspoons of the mirin in a small bowl. Rub the mixture over the cut side of the tomatoes, then place the tomatoes on the baking tray and roast on the middle shelf of the oven for 30 minutes, or until dried out slightly, lightly caramelised and softened.

In a bowl, mix together the remaining miso paste and mirin, the sesame paste, vinegar, sake and soy sauce. Strain the soup mixture through a fine sieve, reserving the mushrooms, and discarding the remaining ingredients. Return the broth to the pan with the sesame paste mixture and mushrooms. Bring to just below a simmer over medium–low heat, then reduce the heat to low and keep warm for 20 minutes to allow the flavours to develop.

Meanwhile, bring a large saucepan of water to the boil and cook the noodles according to the packet instructions.

Divide the noodles, broth and mushrooms among four serving bowls. Top with the roasted tomatoes, boiled eggs and nori, sprinkle with the sesame salt and spring onion and serve immediately.

TOP TIP
• To make a dashi stock from scratch, soak some dried kombu seaweed
  with the dried shiitake mushrooms in 4 cups (1 litre) water for 1 hour.

**HEALTHY FATS
HIGH IN PROTEIN**

• Almost 1½ serves protein per serve
• 36% RDI iodine + over 25% RDI folate
(mostly from sesame) + 15% RDI calcium per serve
• Good source of vitamins C and E
• Good source of fibre and iron (from sesame)

PESCATARIAN • DAIRY FREE • GLUTEN FREE • EGG FREE

FISH BALL LAKSA Serves 4

Laksa soup and fish balls each have a place in my childhood. Laksa was a treat I always looked forward to, while those bouncy, processed, firm-textured fish balls were added by my mum to her home-made soups, often when I was home from school feeling unwell. To my alarm, I recently read the ingredients on a packet of fish balls, which prompted me to create my own, and which I've now incorporated into one of my all-time favourite soups — laksa! If you don't have time to make the fish balls, you can easily replace them with 250 g (9 oz) prawn meat, cutting the prawns in half lengthways before cooking them in the soup.

**2 1/2
SERVES VEG
per serve**

¾ cup (185 g) laksa paste (see tips)
400 ml (14 fl oz) tin coconut milk
4 cups (1 litre) Chicken stock
    (page 220) or Mushroom stock
    (page 216)
400 g (14 oz) peeled pumpkin,
    cut into 2.5 cm (1 inch) pieces
1 zucchini (courgette)
½ quantity Fish balls mixture
    (page 230), rolled into 24 balls,
    about 2.5 cm (1 inch) in size
3⅓ cups (200 g) small broccoli florets
    (see tips)
200 g (7 oz) tofu puffs, halved
200 g (7 oz) dried rice vermicelli
    noodles
1–2 spring onions (scallions), thinly
    sliced on an angle (optional)
coriander (cilantro) sprigs, to serve
lime cheeks, to serve

Heat a large saucepan over medium heat. Cook the laksa paste for 1 minute, or until fragrant, stirring constantly. Stir in the coconut milk and stock and bring to a simmer. Add the pumpkin and cook for 5 minutes.

Meanwhile, slice lengthways around the zucchini, leaving the seeds in the centre, then cut the seedy centre bits into 1 cm (½ inch) pieces. Cut the edges into zucchini noodles, or 'zoodles'. (Alternatively, you can use a julienne peeler or spiraliser if you have one.)

Add the fish balls to the pan, return to a simmer, then add the zucchini pieces, broccoli and tofu puffs. Cook for 5 minutes, or until the fish balls are cooked through and the vegetables are tender.

Meanwhile, prepare the noodles according to the packet instructions, stirring in the zoodles for the last 1 minute, before draining.

Divide the noodle mixture among serving bowls. Ladle in the soup. Top with the spring onion, if using, and serve immediately, with coriander sprigs and lime.

TOP TIPS

- There are many different brands of laksa paste, so follow the packet instructions on your favourite variety as a flavour guide and adjust the quantity accordingly.
- If you're making the Fish balls on page 230 from scratch, you can use the leftover broccoli stems in them instead of green beans.

HIGH IN PROTEIN

- 2 serves protein per serve
- 200% RDI vitamin B12 + 100% RDI vitamin A (from pumpkin, carrot, broccoli) per serve
- Great source of magnesium and vitamin B$_3$
- Good source of iron and fibre

SINGAPORE CHILLI CABB Serves 4

I sure do love Singapore chilli crab. The difficulty of eating it can turn a lot of people off, so here's an easier-to-eat version featuring all the same flavours, a mix of seafood, plus a whole lot of veg (including surprisingly delicious cabbage — hence the name). You would typically serve real Singapore chilli crab with some deep-fried sweet mantou buns to mop up the sauce, but spelt roti is the perfect accompaniment for this one. If you prefer, you can serve with rice vermicelli or egg noodles instead.

2 SERVES VEG per serve

500 g (1 lb 2 oz) clams (vongole), pippies or mussels, scrubbed clean

500 g (1 lb 2 oz) wombok (Chinese cabbage), coarsely chopped

150 g (5½ oz) cavolo nero (Tuscan cabbage) or kale leaves

3 spring onions (scallions), cut into 2 cm (¾ inch) lengths (optional)

250 g (9 oz) baby bok choy, leaves and stems separated

1 tablespoon cornflour

200 g (7 oz) crabmeat, or prawn meat

¾ cup (185 g) Chunky tomato ketchup (page 226); see tip

2 tablespoons kecap manis

1–2 tablespoons fish sauce, to taste

Spelt roti (page 201), to serve

Chilli and lemongrass paste

2–3 long red chillies, finely chopped

2 garlic cloves, crushed or finely chopped

1 lemongrass stem, white part only, finely grated

1 red Asian shallot, coarsely chopped

1 tablespoon finely grated fresh galangal or ginger

2 tablespoons neutral-flavoured oil, such as rice bran or grapeseed oil

½ teaspoon sea salt

Using a stick blender, blend the chilli paste ingredients in a jug. (Alternatively, you can use a blender or small food processor, or you can chop all the ingredients together by hand.)

Heat a wok or large deep frying pan over medium–high heat. Stir-fry the spice paste for 3 minutes. Stir in the clams, wombok, cavolo nero, spring onion and bok choy stems. Cook for 1–2 minutes, then cover for 1 minute, or until the clams just start to open.

In a small bowl, whisk the cornflour with 1 tablespoon water until smooth, then add to the wok with the crabmeat, tomato sauce, kecap manis and fish sauce.

Stir-fry for a further 2 minutes, or until all the ingredients are heated through and the sauce has thickened slightly.

Serve immediately, with roti.

TOP TIP

- If using a store-bought tomato sauce, start off with 3 tablespoons and adjust from there, as commercially made tomato sauce or ketchup contains more sugar and will be much sweeter.

HIGH IN PROTEIN

- 2½ serves wholegrains + ½ serve protein per serve
- Great source of iron (mostly from spelt flour)
- Great source of iodine + selenium

CHICK-IN SCHNITZELS Serves 4

When I first made this recipe, it took me about three days to get over the experience. So meaty in texture, on account of the mushrooms, and still crumbed — it felt like the real chicken schnitzel deal, despite containing minimal meat. For many kids, mushrooms aren't high on the list of go-to vegetables, but sneak them into dishes like this and they won't suspect a thing. I often serve these schnitzels with mash and gravy in the cooler months, and a cabbage slaw once it starts to warm up outside. If you really want to go all out, serve it with both! If you haven't made up any chicken stuffing, you could shred some store-bought barbecued chicken.

6 1/2
SERVES VEG
per serve

8 extra-large portobello or flat
   mushrooms, stems removed
   (see tips)
olive oil or neutral-flavoured oil,
   for drizzling and shallow-frying
½ quantity Chicken stuffing (page 219)
2 eggs
plain flour, for dusting
3 cups (180 g) fresh breadcrumbs
½ cup (120 g) Mayo (page 192)
1 tablespoon white wine vinegar
4 cups (300 g) finely shredded green
   or red cabbage (or a combination)
1 carrot, coarsely grated
Roasted potato mash (page 218),
   to serve
hot Chicken gravy (page 221)
   or Mushroom gravy (page 217),
   to serve

Preheat the grill (broiler) to high and line a large baking tray with foil. Arrange the mushrooms on the tray, drizzle on both sides with oil and season with sea salt and freshly ground black pepper. Grill the mushrooms for 5 minutes on each side, or until golden and cooked, then set aside until cool enough to handle.

Choose four pairs of mushrooms that match each other well in size. Sandwich the pairs together, with the insides facing in, and gently squeeze them together to remove any excess liquid.

Open the mushroom pairs out again. Spread 2 tablespoons of the chicken stuffing over each bottom half. Top with their matched halves and squeeze the pairs together to create a seal and completely enclose the filling.

Preheat the oven to 120°C (235°F). Meanwhile, lightly beat the eggs in a wide shallow bowl. Put the flour and breadcrumbs in separate bowls.

Pour enough oil into a large frying pan to come 2.5 cm (1 inch) up the side. Heat the oil to 180°C (350°F), or until a cube of bread dropped into the oil turns golden brown in 15 seconds.

Working in batches, dust each mushroom 'sandwich' in the flour, shaking off any excess, then dip into the egg until well coated. Coat well in the breadcrumbs.

In batches, cook the schnitzels for 3 minutes on each side, or until golden. Keep warm in the oven while cooking the remaining schnitzels.

Meanwhile, in a large bowl, mix together the mayo and vinegar. Add the cabbage and carrot and toss thoroughly. Season with salt and pepper.

Serve the schnitzels hot, with the slaw, mash and gravy.

TOP TIPS

- You can 'pop' out the mushroom stems in one hit, by 'clicking' or 'flicking' them out. I usually chop and sauté them, then add them to the gravy.
- For a vegan meal, leave the chicken out of the stuffing, and just add the herb mixture from the stuffing on page 219. Serve with mushroom gravy.
- For dairy free, use olive oil rather than butter in the gravy and stuffing.
- For gluten free, use gluten-free flour and breadcrumbs here, and in the gravy.

HIGH IN PROTEIN

- Almost 1 serve protein per serve
- Great source of potassium and iron
- Great source of vitamins B_3, B_{12} and C

THE BURGER Serves 4

This burger is epic. It may be dairy free (though it doesn't have to be), but it certainly isn't lacking in flavour or 'wow' factor. There aren't many burgers that are so packed with veg and antioxidants, as well as protein! If you really want to indulge and serve this burger with chips, I think parsnip chips are always a good option. Add them and you'll get 20% RDI calcium (mostly from the parsnips) in every serve.

2+
SERVES VEG
per serve

4 tablespoons Mayo (page 192)
1 small French shallot, thinly sliced
1 tablespoon olive oil, plus extra
    for drizzling
4 cheese slices, either dairy-free or
    cheddar
4 Milk buns (page 202); see tips
4 iceberg lettuce 'steaks', cut about
    2 cm (¾ inch) thick
sliced pickles, to serve (optional)
Chunky tomato ketchup (page 226),
    to serve

Beef, bean and walnut patties
300 g (10½ oz) minced beef
400 g (14 oz) tin kidney beans, drained
    well, but not rinsed (the residual
    aquafaba will help the patties adhere)
½ cup (50 g) walnuts, finely chopped
1 small zucchini (courgette), coarsely
    grated (optional), excess liquid
    squeezed out
1 garlic clove, finely chopped
    or crushed
2 teaspoons worcestershire sauce
½ teaspoon sea salt

Combine the mayo and shallot in a small bowl and set aside to let the oniony flavour soften.

Put the patty ingredients in a bowl and season with freshly ground black pepper. Using your hands, mix together until very well combined. Shape the mixture into four patties about 2.5 cm (1 inch) thick, and the same diameter as your buns.

Heat the oil in a large frying pan over medium heat. Cook the burger patties for 4 minutes, then turn them over and top each with a slice of cheese. Cook for a further 4 minutes, or until the cheese has melted and the patties are nicely browned and cooked through.

Meanwhile, preheat the grill (broiler) to high. Cut the buns in half and toast them, cut side up, under the grill for 1–2 minutes, or until golden.

Spread the shallot mayo on the base of the buns. Top with the lettuce, burger patties and pickles, if using. Add a dollop of ketchup, then top with the bun lids.

Serve immediately.

TOP TIPS

- You can use store-bought milk buns or other burger buns if you're short on time. Depending on how fresh they are, you may want to wrap them in foil and warm them through, to allow them to soften completely, rather than grilling them on their cut side.
- To make parsnip chips, peel 800 g (1 lb 12 oz) parsnips and cut into chips, discarding the cores. Arrange on a baking tray lined with baking paper and roast in a preheated 220°C (425°F) oven for 20 minutes, or until tender.

HEALTHY FATS
HIGH IN PROTEIN

- 2 serves protein + ½ serve legumes per serve
- Great source of vitamin B$_{12}$
- Good source of iron and vitamin C

MAKE AHEAD
You can make the buns and burger patties in advance. Wrap them individually, and well. The burger patties can be frozen for up to 3 months, and the buns for up to 6 months.

SHEPHERD'S MOUSSAKA Serves 4–6

I've been at it again, combining some favourite childhood dishes of mine. I always loved my mum's shepherd's pie, but I also loved the topping and the eggplant in moussaka... so why not combine the two and throw in some bolognese sauce as well? I always keep some home-made bolognese in the freezer, as it's just so handy for dishes such as this.

8 SERVES VEG per serve

olive oil, for drizzling

2 eggplants (aubergines), cut into 1 cm (½ inch) thick rounds

1 quantity Bolognese sauce (page 210), made with lamb

½ teaspoon ground cinnamon (optional)

1 tablespoon worcestershire sauce (optional)

1 cup (150 g) frozen peas

½ quantity (600 ml) White sauce (page 193)

¼ cup (20 g) finely grated parmesan cheese (optional)

rocket (arugula) leaves, to serve (optional)

Preheat the grill (broiler) to high. Line a large baking tray with foil, drizzle with oil, then arrange half the eggplant slices on the baking tray, in a single layer. Drizzle the eggplant with oil and season with sea salt and freshly ground black pepper. Grill for 10 minutes, or until golden and tender. Remove and set aside, then repeat with the remaining eggplant.

Meanwhile, put the bolognese sauce in a saucepan. Stir in the cinnamon and the worcestershire sauce, if using, and gently warm through. Keep warm over medium–low heat.

Line the base of a greased 8–10 cup (2–2.5 litre) baking dish with half the eggplant. Stir the peas into the bolognese mixture, then transfer to the baking dish, evenly spreading out the mixture. Cover with the remaining eggplant slices, then the white sauce. Sprinkle the cheese over, if using.

Cook under the grill for 10 minutes, or until lightly golden on top. Set aside to rest for 5 minutes, then serve with rocket, if desired.

TOP TIP

- If you're not fond of eggplant, you could use 2 large potatoes instead. Cut them into slices 3 mm (⅛ inch) thick and grill in the same way as the eggplant, but for only 6 minutes, or until tender.
- For a gluten-free moussaka, omit the worcestershire sauce.
- For a dairy-free meal, when making the white sauce, use olive oil instead of butter and omit the cheese, leaving it out of the moussaka as well.

DIVIDE AND CONQUER

- You can make half (or all) the moussaka vegan, using the Vegan mushroom bolognese (see tips, page 211). Omit the cheese, as well as the worcestershire sauce as it contains fish. When making the white sauce, use olive oil instead of butter and omit the cheese. Keep the vegan and meat mixtures separate and assemble as individual serves in heatproof bowls, then grill in exactly the same way.

**HEALTHY FATS
HIGH IN PROTEIN**

- 1½ serves protein + ½ serve legumes per serve
- Richest source of fibre in this book (21 g per serve)
- Good source of calcium (half from plant-based foods)
- Great source of vitamin B_3, C, E and iron (mostly from lentils)
- Loaded with antioxidants

FIT-FOR-AN-ARMY EGGPLANT PARMI Serves 4

What is it about crumbed steaks? Or crumbed anything? They say that texture, and in this case crunch, is more important than taste — so if you're trying to come around to the idea of eggplant, here's a great place to start: crunchy on the outside, and pillowy soft inside. Eggplant usually sucks up a load of oil during frying, so another brilliant thing about this recipe is that the eggplant is baked, for a healthier result.

just under
3
SERVES VEG
per serve

2 eggplants (aubergines), preferably wider ones, rather than taller skinny ones, for a better 'steak' shape

2 eggs

4 tablespoons wholemeal plain flour

2 cups (125 g) fresh breadcrumbs

1 tablespoon finely chopped rosemary

2 tablespoons finely grated parmesan cheese (optional)

4 tablespoons extra virgin oil

1 tablespoon baby capers, patted dry with paper towel (optional)

400 ml (14 fl oz) Roasted tomato passata (page 207), or store-bought tomato passata (puréed tomatoes)

100 g (3½ oz) English spinach, washed well, finely shredded

⅓ cup (60 g) pitted green olives, halved (optional)

4 balls of bocconcini cheese, flattened slightly (to help them melt through quickly)

rocket (arugula) leaves, to serve (optional)

Preheat the oven to 200°C (400°F). Line a large baking tray with baking paper.

Remove 2 cm (¾ inch) from the opposite 'cheeks' of each eggplant, then cut each eggplant in half lengthways to make two 'steaks'. Cut the sliced eggplant cheeks into 1.5 cm (⅝ inch) chunks and set aside.

Whisk the eggs in a wide, shallow bowl. Put the flour in another bowl and season with sea salt and freshly ground black pepper. In another wide shallow bowl, combine the breadcrumbs, rosemary and parmesan, if using, then rub in 3 tablespoons of the oil with your fingertips until it coats the breadcrumbs. Season with salt and pepper.

Dust each cut side of the eggplant steaks with flour, leaving the skin uncoated. Shake off any excess flour, then dip each cut side into the egg, leaving the skin uncoated, and then into the breadcrumb mixture until well coated.

Place the 'schnitzels' on the baking tray, narrower side facing up. Bake for 20–25 minutes, or until golden and cooked through.

Meanwhile, heat the remaining 1 tablespoon oil in a wide deep frying pan over medium–high heat. Add the chopped eggplant cheeks, and the capers if using, and cook for 3 minutes, or until lightly golden. Reduce the heat to medium, stir in the passata and bring to a simmer. Add the spinach and olives, if using. Stir occasionally for 2 minutes, or until the spinach wilts; keep warm over low heat.

Just before serving, add the bocconcini to the pan of passata, leaving enough space in between each one to allow for easier removal. Warm through for about 1 minute, or until the cheese has just melted.

Place an eggplant parmigiana on each serving plate, then spoon each bocconcini mound over the centre. Spoon over the sauce and serve immediately, with rocket leaves, if desired.

TOP TIPS

- **To make the dish dairy free, omit the parmesan and bocconcini.**
- **For gluten-free parmigiana, use gluten-free flour and breadcrumbs.**

HEALTHY FATS

- Over 1 serve wholegrains per serve
- Almost 50% RDI calcium per serve
- Very high in fibre (mostly from eggplant)
- Good source of vitamin A

VEGAN-ABLE • DAIRY FREE • GLUTEN FREE • NUT FREE • EGG FREE

SEAFOOD PIE-AY-YA! Serves 4

There are so many variations of this Spanish one-pan wonder. You'll find this one is packed full of flavour and super easy to prepare. You can vary the fish and seafood to suit your family's taste.

**over
2¹/2
SERVES VEG
per serve**

1 tablespoon extra virgin olive oil, plus extra to serve

1 red capsicum (pepper), cut into small chunks

200 ml (7 fl oz) Roasted tomato passata (page 207), or store-bought tomato passata (puréed tomatoes)

1 tablespoon smoked paprika

a pinch of saffron threads (optional), soaked in 1 tablespoon warm water

3 cups (750 ml) Chicken stock (page 220) or Mushroom stock (page 216)

1 cup (220 g) calasparra, bomba, arborio or Japanese short-grain rice

1 baby fennel bulb, quartered and thinly sliced

1 cup (125 g) green beans, trimmed and cut into thirds

8 raw prawns, peeled and deveined

300 g (10½ oz) fish, such as firm white fish or salmon, bones removed, cut into 3 cm (1¼ inch) cubes

½ cup (75 g) frozen peas, thawed in a bowl of boiling water

½ cup (120 g) marinated artichokes, cut into bite-sized pieces

4 tablespoons coarsely chopped parsley (optional)

lemon wedges, to serve

Heat the oil in a paella pan or large wide frying pan measuring about 35 cm (14 inches) over medium heat. Add the capsicum and cook, stirring, for 3 minutes. Stir in the passata and paprika until combined, along with the saffron and its soaking liquid, if using. Season with sea salt and freshly ground black pepper and cook for a further 5 minutes, or until the passata has reduced and thickened.

Stir in the stock and bring to a simmer. Stir in the rice to combine, then do not stir the rice again. Reduce the heat to medium–low.

Scatter the fennel over the top and cook for 5 minutes. Add the green beans and cook for 5 minutes, then add the prawns and fish and cook for a further 5 minutes.

Scatter the peas and artichokes over and cook for a further 3 minutes, or until the rice is al dente and the fish and prawns are just cooked.

Sprinkle with the parsley, if using, and serve with lemon wedges and an extra drizzle of olive oil.

TOP TIPS

- Don't be daunted if you don't have a paella pan; the recipe also works well in a wide heavy-based frying pan that isn't too thick.
- Saffron is a very expensive spice, but a little goes a long way. It's not essential for this dish, but definitely worth using.

DIVIDE AND CONQUER

- You can easily make this paella vegan by using mushroom stock, and omitting the seafood or cooking it separately for the pescatarians.

**HEALTHY FATS
HIGH IN PROTEIN
LOW SATURATED FAT**

- 1 serve protein per serve
- High in dietary fibre and vitamin C
- Good source of folate (mostly from capsicum, artichokes, tomato, then fennel)
- No added sugars

DAIRY FREEABLE • GLUTEN FREEABLE • NUT FREE

SERIOUS SWEDISH MEATBALLS Serves 4

Ah, to visit IKEA and get a plate of Swedish meatballs. It's a thing! But here's another fine thing to get your teeth into, as these meatballs are loaded with good stuff, especially vegetables — and this meal has over six serves of veg in every serve. This is my ultimate mix of vegies, but you can switch things up, by leaving the green beans out, for example, or swapping the cabbage for another vegetable, and serving the lingonberry jam on the side rather than tossing it through the cabbage.

over 6 SERVES VEG per serve

300 g (10½ oz) minced beef, or a mix
    of pork and veal
200 g (7 oz) broccoli, finely chopped
    using a food processor, or grated
    and finely chopped
2 garlic cloves, finely chopped
2 spring onions (scallions), finely
    chopped
2 tablespoons finely chopped dill
½ teaspoon mixed spice, or ¼ teaspoon
    each ground nutmeg and allspice
1 egg
½ cup (30 g) fresh breadcrumbs,
    such as gluten-free or spelt
2 tablespoons olive oil, plus extra
    for drizzling
750 g (1 lb 10 oz) red cabbage,
    finely shredded
3–4 tablespoons lingonberry,
    redcurrant or cranberry jam or sauce
3 tablespoons red wine vinegar
    or white wine vinegar
300 g (10½ oz) green beans, trimmed
Roasted potato mash (page 218),
    to serve (see tip)
warm Gravy, such as Chicken
    (page 221), Mushroom (page 217)
    or Beef (page 225)

Preheat the oven to 220°C (425°F). Line a baking tray with baking paper.

Place the minced meat, broccoli, garlic, spring onion, dill, mixed spice, egg and breadcrumbs in a bowl and season well with sea salt and ground white or black pepper. Using your hands, mix together well, then roll into 3–4 cm (1¼–1½ inch) balls; you should end up with 16–20 meatballs.

Arrange the meatballs along one side of the baking tray, drizzle with oil and season with salt and pepper. Bake for 10 minutes, then remove the meatballs from the tray and set aside. Leave the oven on.

Meanwhile, heat 1 tablespoon of the oil in a deep frying pan or saucepan over medium–high heat. Add the cabbage and 3 tablespoons water and cook, stirring often, for 5 minutes. Season with salt and pepper, stir in the lingonberry jam and vinegar and cook for a further 5 minutes, stirring until tender. Keep warm over low heat.

Heat the remaining 1 tablespoon oil in a large frying pan over medium heat. Cook the meatballs for 5 minutes, or until evenly golden, turning often.

Meanwhile, add the green beans to the same baking tray the meatballs were on. Lightly drizzle with oil, season with salt and pepper, then roast for 5 minutes, or until tender.

Serve the meatballs with the mash, green beans, cabbage and gravy.

TOP TIPS

- When making the Roasted potato mash, cover the potatoes in foil and bake them on one side of the tray with the meatballs for 10 minutes. Remove the meatballs from the tray and set aside, then remove the foil from the potatoes and bake them, uncovered, for a further 10–15 minutes, until tender — then continue as per the mash recipe on page 218.
- To make this dish vegetarian, use the Vego balls on page 227 instead of the meatballs, and serve with mushroom gravy.
- For dairy free, use olive oil when making the mash and gravy.
- For gluten free, use gluten-free flour and crumbs, here and in the gravy.

**HEALTHY FATS
HIGH IN PROTEIN**

- 1 serve protein + over 50% RDI folate per serve
- Great source of fibre and vitamin B_{12}
- Great source of vitamin C (mostly from cabbage)
- Good source of iron

CHAPTER FOUR

GET DESSERTED

BETTER CHOCOLATE BROWNIES Makes 15 pieces

Not only are these some of the healthiest brownies around, they're also delicious, with the cooked beetroot giving them a jelly-like texture. Compared to your standard brownies, these have only 65 per cent of the calories, 40 per cent of the cholesterol, less than a third of the carbs, more than double the fibre *and* less than a third of the sugars. A commercial brownie square has 6 extra teaspoons of sugar, too!

> just under
> **1/2**
> **SERVE VEG**
> per serve

1 cup (150 g) chopped dark chocolate (70% cacao)

50 g (1¾ oz) butter, or 50 ml (1¾ fl oz) coconut oil

50 ml (1¾ fl oz) extra virgin olive oil or coconut oil

3 eggs

½ cup (50 g) walnuts, coarsely chopped

½ cup (125 ml) maple syrup

3 tablespoons unsweetened cocoa powder, plus extra for dusting

250 g (9 oz) cooked beetroot, coarsely grated

¾ cup (100 g) finely grated zucchini (courgette)

2 cups (230 g) LSA (ground linseed, sunflower seed and almond mix)

2 teaspoons baking powder

2 teaspoons natural vanilla extract

a large pinch of sea salt

Preheat the oven to 170°C (325°F). Line a 30 × 20 cm (12 × 8 inch) baking tin with baking paper.

Place ⅔ cup (100 g) of the chocolate in a large microwave-safe bowl. Add the butter and olive oil. Microwave in 30-second increments until the ingredients have melted, stirring with a metal spoon in between. Allow to cool slightly.

Whisk in the eggs, then stir in the remaining ingredients until well combined.

Pour the mixture into the baking tin and bake for 20–25 minutes, or until a skewer comes out with a few moist crumbs attached.

Set aside on a rack to cool, before cutting into 15 pieces. Dust with extra cocoa powder to serve.

TOP TIP

- **For vegan or dairy-free brownies, use coconut oil instead of butter, and check the chocolate is also dairy free.**

HEALTHY FATS
HIGH IN PROTEIN
LOW CARB

- 1 serve protein per serve
- Good source of magnesium

MAKE AHEAD
You can store the brownies in an airtight container in the fridge for up to 5 days, or wrap them individually and freeze for up to 6 months.

VEGETARIAN • GLUTEN FREE • NUT FREE • EGG FREE

BANOFFEE ICE CREAM Makes about 4 cups (1 litre)

This super-dooper no-churn ice cream is sure to please. Using very ripe bananas, freezing them in their skins, and then allowing them to thaw really helps draw out and accentuate their flavour, though it's not absolutely necessary to do this. Using my yoghurt-based sour-ish cream gives a rich and satisfying result.

4 very ripe bananas, frozen, then
   thawed
2 cups (550 g) Sour-ish cream
   (page 192)
1 quantity Salted caramel (page 197)
2 teaspoons natural vanilla extract
2 tablespoons maple syrup, or to taste
   (optional)

Blend all the ingredients in a blender or food processor until very smooth. Pour the mixture into a 4 cup (1 litre) container and chill in the freezer for 4 hours, or until set.

Remove from the freezer about 10 minutes before serving, to soften.

TOP TIP

- You will always lose some sweetness on freezing, so keep this in mind when tasting your mixture before putting it in the freezer. If it tastes perfectly sweet, you may still need to add 1–2 tablespoons maple syrup to keep it that way. The final flavour will also depend on the sweetness of your bananas and dates, and the tartness of your sour-ish cream.

- 1½ serves fruit per serve
- Only ½ teaspoon added sugars per serve
- Good source of calcium and potassium

MAKE AHEAD
The ice cream will keep in an airtight container
in the freezer for up to 6 months.

SWEET CORN DOUGHNUTS Makes 12

Okey dokey. These are balls of rich deliciousness — and knowing they also have vegetables and wholegrains in every bite will make you feel good about enjoying a taste of pure indulgence.

1/2 SERVE VEG per doughnut

2 teaspoons instant dried yeast
1 tablespoon caster sugar
¾ cup (110 g) wholemeal plain flour
¾ cup (80 g) almond meal
¼ teaspoon sea salt
1 egg
4 tablespoons milk or non-dairy milk
½ cup (125 g) Sweet creamed corn (page 214)
½ cup (80 g) corn kernels (about ½ cob)
neutral-flavoured oil, such as rice bran or pure vegetable oil, for deep-frying
icing (confectioners') sugar, for dusting

Brown butter maple glaze
25 g (1 oz) butter
4 tablespoons maple syrup
a large pinch of sea salt

Put the yeast in a small bowl with ½ teaspoon of the sugar and 3 tablespoons lukewarm water. Stir to combine, then set aside for 5 minutes, or until the mixture has developed bubbles.

Combine the remaining sugar in a large bowl with the flour, almond meal and salt. Make a well in the centre.

Lightly beat the egg in a large jug, then whisk in the milk, creamed corn and corn kernels to combine.

Pour the corn mixture into the well in the dry ingredients, along with the yeast mixture, and start to mix from the centre of the bowl, incorporating the flour mixture. Set aside to prove in a warm draught-free place for 1 hour, or until doubled in size.

Pour enough oil into a saucepan to come one-third of the way up the side (I use a medium-sized pan, so I don't have to add too much oil). Heat the oil to 180°C (350°F), or until a cube of bread dropped into the oil turns golden brown in 15 seconds.

Using two dessert spoons, scoop up some dough with one spoon, then use the second spoon to carefully scrape off the mixture in a ball, into the oil. Cook the doughnuts in batches for 4 minutes, or until golden and cooked through, turning regularly; I usually cook the doughnuts in three batches, four at a time. Remove with a slotted spoon and drain well on paper towel.

Meanwhile, to make the glaze, brown the butter in a small saucepan over medium heat until it is golden brown and has a nutty aroma, swirling the pan. Add the maple syrup and salt and stir to combine, then pour into a large bowl.

Coat the doughnuts lightly in the glaze, making sure you don't douse them, or there won't be enough for all of them. Sift some icing sugar over the top. The doughnuts are best served warm.

TOP TIPS

• When cooking the doughnuts it's best not to overcrowd the pan, so the oil temperature doesn't drop too much, or the doughnuts will soak up the oil.
• For dairy-free doughnuts, omit the brown butter maple glaze, and instead dust them with icing sugar after lightly drizzling with maple syrup.

• ½ serve wholegrains per serve
• ½ serve protein per serve

SWEET STRAWBERRY SHORTCAKE Serves 8

I may be seen as a party pooper who cuts out all the fun of birthdays by making a healthier cake alternative, but I made this cake for my daughter's second birthday because she loves strawberries so much and it went down a treat! The cakey bits that are cooked on the side were an accidental success: I had too much batter for the cake tin, so I thought I'd bake it anyway and it worked.

1/4 SERVE VEG per serve

400 g (14 oz) tin chickpeas, drained
1 cup (150 g) spelt or wholemeal flour
1 tablespoon baking powder
½ cup (60 g) icing (confectioners')
   sugar mixture
a large pinch of sea salt
100 g (3½ oz) butter, plus extra
   for greasing
1 egg
½ cup (135 g) Sour-ish cream
   (page 192)
400 g (14 oz) strawberries, larger ones
   halved

Red berry drizzle
½ cup (50 g) fresh or frozen
   raspberries
100 g (3½ oz) strawberries, coarsely
   chopped
1 tablespoon maple syrup

Maple vanilla whip
1½ cups (400 g) Sour-ish cream
   (page 192)
4 tablespoons maple syrup
2 teaspoons natural vanilla extract

Preheat the oven to 200°C (400°F). Grease a 6 cm (2½ inch) deep round cake tin, measuring 24 cm (9½ inches) across the base, and line the base with baking paper. Line a separate baking tray with baking paper.

Using a stick blender or small food processor, purée the chickpeas until smooth.

In a large bowl, combine the flour, baking powder, icing sugar mixture and salt. Using your fingertips, rub the butter and chickpea paste into the flour mixture until it resembles breadcrumbs.

Whisk the egg and sour-ish cream in a jug until combined. Add to the flour mixture and gently mix until just combined.

Place three-quarters of the dough in the cake tin, spreading it out evenly using a palette knife or the back of spoon. Put the remaining dough on the lined baking tray and smooth it out to about 2.5 cm (1 inch) thick; it can be a rough shape as it's going to be broken up when assembling the cake.

Bake for 15–20 minutes, or until the cakes are golden and a skewer inserted in the centre of the main cake comes out clean. Stand for 5 minutes before turning the cakes out onto a wire rack to cool.

Blend the red berry drizzle ingredients until smooth.

In a separate bowl, whisk the maple vanilla whip ingredients to combine.

Place the main cake on a serving platter. Break the smaller cake into large pieces. Layer the surface of the main cake with dollops of the maple vanilla whip, smaller cake pieces and strawberries. Drizzle with the red berry drizzle to serve.

This cake is best made near serving time, as it doesn't store too well.

• Almost 1 serve wholegrains per serve
• ¼ serve protein per serve
• ¼ serve fruit per serve

CLEAN GREEN ICE BLOCKS
Makes about 750 ml (3 cups)

My daughter devours these nutrient-dense ice blocks. And I love it that I can feel good about giving her one as a treat. Fluoro lime-green ice blocks were always my favourite as a kid, so it's only fitting that I keep these ones green as well. The avocado and coconut flesh lend a lovely creaminess that is light and refreshing.

about
1/4
SERVE VEG
per serve

1 young coconut, or 350 ml (12 fl oz)
    coconut water
1 ripe avocado
1 small Lebanese cucumber, coarsely
    chopped
½ small green apple, peeled and cored,
    coarsely chopped
1 tablespoon mint leaves (optional)
3 tablespoons coarsely chopped
    spinach (optional)
1 tablespoon lime juice
3–4 tablespoons maple syrup, to taste
a pinch of sea salt

Crack open the coconut, if using, and pour the juice into a blender. Using a spoon, scoop out the flesh from inside the coconut and add to the blender. Alternatively, add the coconut water to the blender.

Add the remaining ingredients and blend until very smooth.

Pour the mixture into ice block (popsicle/ice lolly) moulds, to about 1 cm (½ inch) from the top to allow the mixture to expand as it freezes.

Place in the freezer for about 4 hours, until frozen.

TOP TIP

- You will always lose some sweetness on freezing, so keep this in mind when tasting your mixture before putting it in the freezer. If it tastes perfectly sweet, you may need to add a little more maple syrup than you think you need, to counteract this effect.

HEALTHY FATS
LOW CARB
LOW SATURATED FAT

MAKE AHEAD
You can make extra and freeze your ice blocks
for up to 6 months.

PEAR TATIN PANCAKE Serves 6–8

This has to be one of the ultimate quick-cook cakes around. Although the typical puff pastry version with rich, buttery caramel is simply irresistible on a fruit tatin, this version gives it a good run for its money.

3 tablespoons olive oil or coconut oil

2 firm but ripe pears

½ cup (65 g) buckwheat flour

½ cup (75 g) spelt or wholemeal
   plain flour

2 teaspoons baking powder

¼ teaspoon salt

1 teaspoon ground ginger

½ cup (110 g) caster sugar, or ½ cup
   (125 ml) maple syrup

2 eggs

¾ cup (185 ml) milk of your choice;
   I use 'drinking' coconut milk

50 g (1¾ oz) butter, melted, or
   2½ tablespoons coconut oil

1 vanilla bean, seeds scraped, or
   1 teaspoon natural vanilla extract

Salted caramel (page 197), to serve

Preheat the oven to 180°C (350°F).

Warm the oil in a 22 cm (8½ inch) ovenproof frying pan over medium heat and swirl the pan so the oil coats the base. Remove from the heat.

Peel the pears, cut them lengthways into quarters and remove the cores. Cut each pear quarter into two or three slices, depending on the size of the pears. Arrange the pears around the base of the pan in a flower-like arrangement.

Combine the dry ingredients in a large bowl, including the sugar, if using instead of maple syrup.

In a separate bowl, whisk together the eggs, milk, melted butter, vanilla seeds or vanilla extract, and the maple syrup, if using.

Make a well in the centre of the dry ingredients and pour in the milk mixture. Starting from the centre, whisk the wet mixture into the dry, until just combined. Set aside to rest for 10 minutes.

Evenly pour the batter into the pan over the pears, then place over medium heat for 2 minutes, or until the batter is starting to sizzle and bubble.

Transfer to the oven and bake for 15 minutes, or until the cake is golden and a skewer inserted in the centre comes out clean. Remove from the oven and set aside for 5 minutes.

Meanwhile, heat the caramel sauce until warm.

Using a silicon spatula or something similar, gently check to see if the cake will easily come away from the pan. If it doesn't, you will gently need to lift around the base of the pan with the spatula to help release it.

Place a serving platter upside down on top of the pan, in the centre, then carefully invert the cake onto the platter. Drizzle with the caramel sauce to serve. I like to serve the pear tatin warm, but it is also good cold.

TOP TIPS

- It's best to use a cast-iron enamel or non-stick frying pan, to ensure the cake releases from the pan more easily.
- If you don't have any salted caramel on hand, serve with maple syrup.
- To make the cake dairy free, use coconut oil instead of butter, and a non-dairy milk.
- Use gluten-free flour if you'd like to avoid gluten. Buckwheat is gluten free.

- 1 serve wholegrains per serve
- ½ serve fruit per serve

SALTED CARAMEL THICKSHAKE Serves 4

Oh, the memories. When I was much younger, I must confess that I did love a particular chocolate thickshake and caramel sundae from a certain fast food chain. A friend and I would dunk our fries into the sundae and eat them that way. This thickshake is a remake of those times — but better for you by far.

4 cups (1 litre) milk, such as
    almond milk
½ cup (125 ml) Salted caramel
    (page 197), or more to taste
2 teaspoons natural vanilla extract
    (optional)
1–2 tablespoons maple syrup, to taste
    (optional)
a pinch of sea salt

Pour 600 ml (21 fl oz) of the milk into a shallow container and chill in the freezer at least 4 hours, or overnight, until firm.

When you're ready to serve, break the icy milk mixture up a bit, then put it in a blender with all the remaining ingredients, including the remaining 400 ml (14 fl oz) milk.

Blend until smooth, then serve immediately.

TOP TIPS

- The amount of maple syrup you need will come down to the sweetness of the dates in your salted caramel, and the sweetness of the milk you use. I use almond, soy or 'drinking' coconut milk, so a natural sweetness comes through and find I don't need too much maple syrup, if any at all. If you use dairy milk, you'll need a little more maple syrup.
- For a vegan or dairy-free thickshake, use a plant-based milk.
- For a nut-free thickshake, avoid almond milk.

- 1 serve fruit per serve
- ¼ serve protein per serve

PECAN PUMPKIN PIE Serves 6–8

Pecan meets pumpkin pie: surely a cause for celebration, especially given that this pie isn't full of high-fructose corn syrup or cream. Pumpkin is a source of antioxidants, while pecans provide essential fatty acids, and cinnamon is a blood glucose stabiliser. If your pastry shrinks slightly, don't be disheartened; this is due to the chickpeas in the vegan pastry, rather than your cooking skills. You can certainly use shortcrust pastry instead.

just under
1
SERVE VEG
per serve

1 quantity My shortcrust pastry
   (page 204), chilled
300 g (10½ oz) peeled pumpkin,
   such as jap or kent, cut into 4 cm
   (1½ inch) cubes
2 tablespoons unsalted butter, melted
100 ml (3½ fl oz) maple syrup
2 teaspoons natural vanilla extract
2 teaspoons ground cinnamon
4 eggs

Maple pecans
1¼ cups (125 g) pecans
2½ tablespoons maple syrup

Preheat the oven to 180°C (350°F). Lightly grease a 5–6 cup (1.25–1.5 litre) pie dish.

Roll out the pastry to fit the pie dish, then ease it into the dish and trim the edges. Using a fork, prick holes in the base. Scrunch up a large piece of baking paper and use it to line the pastry. Chill in the freezer until the oven reaches the right temperature.

Remove the dish from the freezer and fill with baking beads or dried pulses. Bake for 15 minutes, then carefully remove the baking beads and baking paper. Return to the oven for a further 10 minutes to dry out the base.

Meanwhile, bring a saucepan of water to the boil. Cook the pumpkin for 10 minutes, or until very tender. Drain in a colander and leave to air-dry.

Purée the pumpkin using a stick blender or food processor. Add the melted butter, maple syrup, vanilla extract, cinnamon, eggs and a large pinch of sea salt and process until smooth. Pour the mixture into the pie base.

Bake for 25 minutes, or until the filling is set, but the centre still wobbles slightly. Remove from the oven and set aside to cool completely.

Meanwhile, put the maple pecan ingredients in a small frying pan with a pinch of sea salt. Cook over medium heat for 3 minutes, stirring constantly, until the pecans are glazed and shiny. Remove from the heat and set aside to cool.

Just before serving, top the pie with the maple pecans.

TOP TIPS

- Don't worry if your maple pecans start crystallising. They will still taste absolutely delicious.
- When blind-baking pastry, it is better to use either baking beads or dried pulses (such as kidney beans) rather than dried rice, to allow the heat to properly get through to the pastry base and dry it out.

- 1 serve protein per serve
- ½ serve legumes per serve

MAKE AHEAD

You can store the pie in an airtight container in the fridge for up to 3 days, but it's best to keep the maple pecans separate and top the pie with them just before serving.

VEGETARIAN • DAIRY FREEABLE • NUT FREE

CORNY CUSTARD TARTS Makes 12

One of my favourite parts of yum cha or dim sum is selecting the wonderfully flaky egg custard tarts to finish off the meal. Here's the version of those tarts that I make at home. Super simple to prepare, these ones have half the sugars and saturated fat of a Chinese custard tart.

**1/4
SERVE VEG
per serve**

cooking oil spray

6–7 sheets filo pastry

¾ cup (185 g) Sweet creamed corn (page 214)

3 eggs, lightly beaten

¾ cup (180 ml) milk of your choice (see tip)

3 tablespoons icing (confectioners') sugar mixture, plus extra for dusting

Preheat the oven to 180°C (350°F). Spray a 12-hole standard muffin tin with oil.

Remove the filo pastry from the packet and cover with a damp tea towel.

Working quickly, making one tart case at a time, cut eight squares from a pastry sheet. Spray the first square well with oil, then place another square on top, about 1 cm (½ inch) to the right. Continue to spray and place squares a little to the right to create a star shape.

Carefully insert the pastry star into a muffin hole and push around the base of the tin only, allowing the pastry sides to curve and fold naturally. Make the remaining 11 tart shells in the same way.

Line each tart shell with scrunched-up squares of baking paper, add baking beads to each, and blind bake for 8–10 minutes, or until the pastry is very lightly golden and starting to crisp.

Remove from the oven and allow to cool slightly.

Whisk the remaining ingredients in a jug until combined. Evenly divide the mixture among the tart shells and bake for a further 12–15 minutes, or until the custard is set and the pastry is crisp.

Remove from the oven and cool slightly on a wire rack to avoid condensation, so the pastry bases stay crisp.

Dust with icing sugar to serve. I like the tarts served warm, but they are also enjoyable when cooled.

TOP TIP

- I tend to use 'drinking' coconut milk when making this recipe, as we usually have it in the fridge — or anything that's a little sweeter, such as soy milk. These are great options if you'd like the tarts to be dairy free, in which case, use olive oil rather than butter in the sweet creamed corn.

**HEALTHY FATS
LOW CARB**

MAKE AHEAD

You can store the tarts in the fridge in an airtight container for 3–5 days. Gently warm in an oven at 100°C (200°F) to crisp up the pastry before serving.

TROPICAL PAVLOVA Serves 6–8

This vegan pavlova is quite the triumph. I'd even go so far as to say I prefer the flavour and texture of a meringue made with aquafaba — the 'bean water' from a tin of chickpeas or beans — over one made with egg whites. Meringue made with aquafaba takes a little more patience and much longer beating, and is rather fragile in comparison with its eggy counterpart, but still turns out crisp and chewy. This meringue doesn't keep very long, and will start to break down quite quickly, so it's best to serve it immediately once assembled.

1 quantity aquafaba, from a 400 g (14 oz) tin of chickpeas or other beans

⅔ cup (140 g) raw caster sugar

2 cups (500 g) thick non-dairy yoghurt, such as coconut yoghurt

1 ripe mango, cheeks removed, thinly sliced

1 large ripe banana, thinly sliced lengthways

¼ papaya, peeled and seeded, thinly sliced

2 passionfruit, halved

Preheat the oven to 150°C (300°F). Line a large baking tray with baking paper; you may need two trays.

Using an electric mixer, whisk the aquafaba to soft peaks, which will take about 10 minutes. Gradually add the sugar, 1 tablespoon at a time, for a further 15 minutes, until the mixture is thick and firm, and the sugar has dissolved.

Spread three-quarters of the mixture on the baking tray, in a free-form rectangle about 3–4 cm (1¼–1½ inches) thick. Dollop the rest of the mixture into smaller meringue drops, either on the side of the same tray if there is room, or on another lined baking tray.

Transfer to the oven and reduce the oven temperature to 120°C (235°F). Bake for 1½ hours, then turn the oven off and leave the meringue in the oven for 4 hours, or overnight, keeping the oven door ajar with a wooden spoon.

Just before serving, place the yoghurt in a bowl and use a whisk to loosen it up. Arrange the fruit slices on the large meringue, layering them with the yoghurt and meringue drops. Dollop with the passionfruit pulp and serve immediately.

TOP TIPS

- Be sure to whip up your aquafaba fresh from the tin for optimal results.
- The meringue mixture will flatten and spread out quite a lot in the oven. This is normal, so don't be alarmed; it will naturally lose some height.
- If your meringue drops end up quite large, you can break them up into smaller bits for serving.
- Top the pavlova with any of your favourite tropical fruits; I also like lychees, thinly sliced fresh pineapple and toasted shredded coconut.

HEALTHY FATS
HIGH IN PROTEIN
LOW CARB

- Just under 1 serve fruit per serve
- The fruit toppings are a great source of antioxidants

SALTED CARAMEL SLICE Makes 18 pieces

I've never really had a sweet tooth, but a sickly sweet caramel slice from the bakery has always been my weakness. When I was pregnant with my daughter, we lived opposite a fabulous ice-cream shop that also sold some incredible desserts. I'd be in there every other day, and the caramel slice trumped every time. It's fair to say that a good portion of the extra 25 kilograms I gained can be attributed to that slice alone. Well here's one that won't blow the health budget. Commercial caramel slices have about ten times the amount of added sugar per serve — but this version has less than half the overall sugars, is higher in vitamins and minerals (including double the magnesium), is much lower in cholesterol and has 75 per cent more fibre!

½ cup (50 g) cashews (see tip)
1 cup (100 g) gluten-free rolled oats
½ cup (75 g) fresh pitted dates
½ cup (50 g) almond meal
½ cup (125 ml) coconut oil
½ cup (45 g) desiccated coconut
75 g (2½ oz) butter
1 quantity Salted caramel (page 197)

Chocolate topping
⅔ cup (100 g) chopped dark chocolate
   (70% cacao)
2 tablespoons coconut oil

Soak the cashews in warm water with a pinch of salt for at least 1 hour.

Preheat the oven to 180°C (350°F). Line a 30 × 20 cm (12 × 8 inch) baking tin with baking paper.

In a food processor, pulse the oats until coarsely chopped. Add the dates and pulse until chopped. Add the almond meal, coconut oil and desiccated coconut and pulse to combine. Push the mixture evenly into the base of the baking tin.

Bake for 8–10 minutes, or until lightly golden.

Meanwhile, blend or process the cashews until finely ground and as smooth as possible. Melt the butter in a small saucepan over medium heat. Swirling the pan, cook for 3 minutes, or until the butter turns golden and has a nutty aroma. Add the caramel and cashews and whisk until hot and well combined, then pour the caramel mixture evenly over the biscuit base.

Bake for 8–10 minutes, or until the caramel is slightly firmer and appears drier on the surface. Remove from the oven and allow to cool, before chilling in the fridge for about 30 minutes.

To make the topping, melt the chocolate and oil in a bowl, either in the microwave in 30-second bursts, or in a heatproof bowl over a saucepan of barely simmering water, stirring with a metal spoon. Set aside until warm to the touch, then pour the mixture over the caramel layer.

Chill in the fridge for about 2 hours, until the topping has set.

Remove the slice from the tin and cut into 18 pieces to serve.

TOP TIP

• The longer you soak your cashews, the better they will blend to a paste. If possible, soak them in a bowl of cold water with a pinch of salt overnight; this process is called activating. If doing it this way, give them a good rinse before blending. If you only have an hour, the warmer the soaking water the better, as the nuts will soften more and blend to a paste more easily.

LOW CARB		MAKE AHEAD
	• ½ serve fruit per serve	You can store the slice in an airtight container
	• Only ½ teaspoon added sugars per serve	in the fridge for up to 5 days.

VEGAN • DAIRY FREE • WHEAT FREE • EGG FREE

APPLE 'CRUMBLE' Serves 4

Meet apple crumble, reimagined. Here we have all the elements of a traditional apple crumble, down to the raisin, cinnamon and apple pieces — except we're serving the apples whole, as an elegantly tender shell for the nutty crumble. Plus, we're only dishing up half the saturated fat of a commercial crumble, and almost half the carbs.

4 green or red apples
(or a combination)
1 tablespoon raisins or currants
½ teaspoon ground cinnamon
1 teaspoon natural vanilla extract
2 teaspoons lemon juice
2¼ tablespoons maple syrup
¾ cup (100 g) mixed nuts, such as
slivered almonds, macadamias,
skinless hazelnuts and pistachios
1 tablespoon shredded coconut
4 tablespoons rolled oats
2 tablespoons coconut oil or butter
coconut yoghurt, to serve

Preheat the oven to 180°C (350°F). Line a large baking tray with baking paper.

Using a sharp knife, cut 1.5 cm (⅝ inch) from the top of each apple; you can either snack on these the apple 'lids', or bake them. Make a slight incision around the centre of each apple, to stop them bursting and collapsing during baking. Remove and discard the cores, using an apple corer if you have one.

Using a thin-edged teaspoon, carefully remove the inside of the apple, leaving 1–1.5 cm (¾ inch) of the 'shell' intact to create a bowl. Cut the carved-out apple bits into 1 cm (½ inch) pieces.

Place the apple pieces in a bowl, along with the raisins, cinnamon, vanilla extract, lemon juice and 1 teaspoon of the maple syrup. Add a pinch of sea salt and mix until well combined. Fill the apples with the mixture, reserving the bowl.

Coarsely chop the nuts and combine in the bowl with coconut, oats, oil, remaining 2 tablespoons maple syrup and a pinch of sea salt.

Individually cover each apple with foil, then place along one side of the baking tray. Tip the nut crumble mixture onto the other side of the tray.

Transfer to the oven and bake for 15 minutes, or until the crumble mixture is golden. Remove the crumble mixture to a bowl.

Remove the foil from the apples, then bake for a further 5 minutes, or until the apples are tender.

Top the apples with the crumble mixture and serve warm or cooled, with coconut yoghurt.

TOP TIP

• If some family members like one apple colour more than another, you can cook a mixture of varieties at the same time, as long as they're the same size. Just be aware that some apples cook at a different rate (e.g. pink ladies can take 25 minutes, but green apples only 20), so you may need to remove some earlier than the others, before they start to soften too much.

HIGH IN PROTEIN

• 1 serve protein per serve
• 1 serve fruit per serve

CHAPTER FIVE

SOME CLEVER ODDS & ENDS

VEGAN • DAIRY FREE • GLUTEN FREE • NUT FREE • EGG FREE

MAYO Makes about 1½ cups (375 ml)

The first time I made this vegan mayo was also the first time I had ever used aquafaba, or 'bean water', as an egg substitute. This mayo may be vegan, but it's also absolutely delicious — in fact my family have come to prefer it over standard mayonnaise. It keeps well and is great to have on hand in the fridge.

3 tablespoons aquafaba (the liquid
   from tinned chickpeas or kidney
   beans)
2 teaspoons dijon mustard
1 teaspoon sea salt
1 tablespoon lemon juice or white wine
   vinegar (or a combination)
¼ teaspoon caster sugar
1 garlic clove, crushed (optional)
300 ml (10½ fl oz) grapeseed oil
   or light olive oil

Put all the ingredients except the oil in a blender or small food processor. Start the machine and gradually pour in the oil until the mixture is white and thickened.
   The mayo will keep in an airtight container in the fridge for up to 1 month.

TOP TIP
- For optimal results, it is best to use fresh aquafaba, from a tin of chickpeas or beans that has just been opened.

VEGETARIAN • GLUTEN FREE • NUT FREE • EGG FREE

SOUR-ISH CREAM Makes about 2 cups (550 g)

When comparing your stock-standard Greek yoghurt with sour cream, you'll find sour cream has nearly twice the total and saturated fat, and half the protein and calcium, leaving this yoghurt-based alternative as the clear winner. See if anyone even picks up that it's not sour cream! Use it as you would regular sour cream, or serve it as a soft strained-yoghurt cheese (known as labneh), which is lovely with savoury breakfast dishes, or even on toast instead of butter or cream cheese.

2 teaspoons fine sea salt
1 kg (2 lb 4 oz) tub of Greek-style
   yoghurt

Mix the salt through the yoghurt directly in the tub, then transfer to a sieve lined with paper towel.
   Cover the surface with another piece of paper towel and sit the sieve inside a bowl. Leave to drain in the fridge for 1–2 days, until the mixture is as thick as sour cream. Discard the liquid.
   Transfer to an airtight container and store in the fridge; the sour cream will keep for up to 1 week.

WHITE SAUCE Makes about 5 cups (1.25 litres)

2
SERVES VEG
per serve

White sauce, or béchamel, is up there for me, but the dishes it finds itself in are usually rich and heavy, and in most cases should only be enjoyed occasionally. This version is rich in veg — not that you can tell by its colour, which is hugely helpful if you're dealing with fussy eaters. Using tofu gives the sauce a lovely creaminess, but if you're really not keen, you can always use cannellini beans.

750 g (1 lb 10 oz) trimmed cauliflower, coarsely chopped, including the stem

2½ tablespoons butter or extra virgin olive oil (or a combination)

1 onion, finely chopped

2 garlic cloves, crushed or finely chopped

300 g (10½ oz) silken tofu, or 2 × 400 g (14 oz) tins cannellini beans, drained well

¼ teaspoon ground white or black pepper

½ cup (50 g) finely grated parmesan, pecorino or provolone cheese (optional)

Process the cauliflower in a food processor until finely chopped. Alternatively, you can finely chop it using a sharp knife. Transfer to a saucepan with 2 cups (500 ml) water, season well with sea salt, cover with a lid and place over medium heat. Cook for 15–20 minutes, or until very tender, stirring occasionally.

Meanwhile, melt the butter in a small frying pan over medium heat. Sauté the onion and garlic for 6–8 minutes, or until golden and softened. Season with more salt, then transfer the mixture to a blender or food processor.

Drain the cauliflower through a fine sieve set over a bowl to collect the liquid. Transfer the cauliflower and ½ cup (125 ml) of the cooking liquid to the blender.

Add the tofu, pepper and cheese, if using, and blend until very smooth. Season to taste with salt and use as recipe directs. The sauce will keep in an airtight container in the fridge for up to 2 days.

TOP TIP

- This sauce thickens quite easily, so you may need to thin it out with milk when using it in some recipes.
- To make the sauce dairy free or vegan, use olive oil instead of butter, and omit the cheese.

LOW CARB

- ½ serve protein per serve
- Great source of vitamin C
- No added sugars

BANG BANG SAUCE Makes about ⅔ cup (170 ml)

I love this sauce so much I could almost drink it. Full of flavour, it is my take on the sauce typically served as part of bang bang chicken, the famous Chinese street-food snack, but it's also a great partner for the Poppin' potato pancakes on page 28, as a sauce with steamed or crispy tofu, and as a noodle salad dressing. It keeps well in the fridge, so you may as well make extra.

3 tablespoons Chinese sesame paste
   or tahini (see tips)
1 tablespoon Chinese black vinegar,
   rice vinegar or malt vinegar
1½ tablespoons light soy sauce
2 teaspoons sesame oil
½ teaspoon chilli oil (optional)
2 tablespoons maple syrup, rice syrup
   or sugar (see tips)

Blend all the ingredients together until smooth, using a stick blender or small blender, adding 2 tablespoons water or more for a thinner consistency if needed. The sauce will keep in an airtight container in the fridge for up to 1 month.

TOP TIPS

- You can find Chinese sesame paste at selected Asian supermarkets. It is made from toasted whole sesame seeds, and has a stronger sesame flavour than tahini, the Middle Eastern sesame paste used in hummus. If you can find it, definitely use Chinese sesame paste here, and in the Ramen on page 147.
- If using sugar rather than maple syrup or rice syrup, you'll need to add a little extra water to thin the sauce out.

TANGY ASIAN DRESSING

This is such a quick and simple dressing, great for all kinds of South East Asian–inspired salads and dishes. You can easily spice it up with some thinly sliced fresh chilli and/or ginger, and some chopped fresh herbs such as coriander (cilantro) or Vietnamese mint.

3 tablespoons fish sauce or soy sauce

2–3 tablespoons finely grated palm sugar (jaggery), or maple syrup, to taste

⅔ cup (170 ml) lime juice

Put all the ingredients in a screw-top jar and attach the lid. Shake until the sugar has dissolved and the flavours are well combined.

The dressing will keep in an airtight container in the fridge for up to 5 days.

TOP TIP

- **To make the dressing vegan, use soy sauce rather than fish sauce.**

APPLE SAUCE Makes 2 cups (500 ml)

Gently baking the apples with the leek and garlic intensifies their flavour. I love this apple sauce with the pork recipe on page 135, but it would also go well with braised lamb. For an added flavour boost, you could stir in ½ teaspoon toasted fennel seeds just after you've puréed the sauce ingredients together.

1 leek, white part only, thinly sliced

2 green apples, unpeeled, quartered, cores removed

2 garlic cloves, unpeeled

extra virgin olive oil, for drizzling

1 tablespoon white wine vinegar or cider vinegar

1½ tablespoons maple syrup, or 2 teaspoons sugar

4 tablespoons coarsely chopped mint

Preheat the oven to 200°C (400°F). Line a baking tray with baking paper.

Put the leek, apples and garlic cloves on the baking tray and drizzle with oil. Season with sea salt and freshly ground black pepper, tossing to coat. Roast for 15 minutes, then remove from the oven.

When the garlic is cool enough to handle, squeeze the flesh from the skins into a small saucepan. Add the roasted leek and apple, along with the vinegar, maple syrup, mint and 1 cup (250 ml) water.

Purée the mixture using a stick blender, then season to taste with more salt and pepper.

Warm over low heat to serve.

½ serve fruit per serve

MAKE AHEAD

You can make the sauce ahead and store in a jar or airtight container in the fridge for up to 1 week.

SALTED CARAMEL Makes about 1 cup (250 ml)

I like to sweeten desserts with dates, as a replacement to refined sugars. Yes, dates are high in natural sugars, but unlike refined sugars, dates are also rich in dietary fibre. As with everything, I think they're fine enjoyed in moderation. I'm sure you'll find many uses for this luscious caramel. I use it in home-made thickshakes and ice creams, and drizzle it over pancakes for a touch of sweet.

12 pitted dates, preferably fresh
270 ml (9½ fl oz) tin coconut cream
½ teaspoon fine sea salt

Using a stick blender or small blender, process all the ingredients until smooth.

Transfer to a small saucepan and cook over low heat, stirring regularly, for 10 minutes.

Use straight away, or store in the fridge and gently reheat in the microwave for serving.

TOP TIP
• You can keep the sauce a little chunky, rather than smooth, if you prefer.

• High in fibre (from the dates)
• No added sugars

MAKE AHEAD
This sauce keeps well, so make a double batch and store in the fridge in a jar or airtight container for up to 1 month.

SCRATCH, CRACKLIN' POP (SESAME RICE CRACKERS) Makes lots

Freshly made sesame salt is the key to these cracking good rice crackers, which taste a bit like pork crackling, but without all the saturated fat — or any pork! You can easily halve this recipe, but the crackers get eaten so quickly I found it's better to make a lot of them, especially if I'm using them in other dishes, such as the roast pork dinner on page 135. It's the sesame seeds that make them taste 'porky', so the toastier and more of them there are, the better. The thinly rolled dough can be a little delicate to handle, but the crackers don't need to be perfectly shaped, so don't worry too much. The thinner you roll the crackers, the quicker they'll cook.

⅔ cup (150 g) short-grain white rice

1 cup (160 g) fine rice flour (see tip)

1½ teaspoons fine sea salt

½ teaspoon bicarbonate of soda (baking soda)

1 tablespoon sesame oil

½ cup (75 g) Sesame salt (page 200) or sesame seeds

1 tablespoon mirin

1 tablespoon gluten-free soy sauce

Rinse the rice well, place in a small saucepan with 1 cup (250 ml) water and cover with a lid. Bring to a simmer over medium heat, then reduce the heat to low and cook for 10–12 minutes, or until the water has been absorbed. Turn off the heat and stand, covered, for 5–10 minutes.

Meanwhile, preheat the oven to 180°C (350°F).

Using a small food processor or stick blender, very finely chop the cooked rice until you have a sticky, relatively smooth paste. Add the rice flour, salt, bicarbonate of soda and sesame oil and process until very well combined; you may need to add a little water, 2 teaspoons at a time. The dough shouldn't be too dry, or too sticky.

Spread the sesame salt on a plate.

For a traditional shape, you can roll the rice dough into 2 cm (¾ inch) balls, coat well in the sesame salt, then roll out between two sheets of baking paper to about 2 mm (¹/₁₆ inch) thick. Alternatively, to make the crackers look more like pork crackling, coat the dough well with the sesame salt, using it all up, then roll out the whole mixture between two sheets of baking paper to a 2 mm (¹/₁₆ inch) thickness. Using a pizza wheel or sharp knife, cut into long shards.

Leaving the crackers on the bottom sheet of baking paper, carefully transfer the sheet to a large baking tray. Bake for 15–20 minutes, or until the crackers are evenly deep golden, switching the trays around halfway through.

Remove the crackers from the oven. Combine the mirin and soy sauce in a bowl and very lightly brush the glaze over both sides of the crackers. Place them on a rack and allow to dry out and cool completely.

The crackers will keep in an airtight container for up to 2 weeks.

TOP TIP

• Use a very fine powdery rice flour, from an Asian grocery store. Supermarket brands can be rather coarse, making your crackers grainy and sandy.

• Great source of vitamin E
• Very low in saturated fat

SESAME SALT   Makes about 1⅔ cups (250 g)

In Japan, sesame salt is known as gomashio. And it's remarkable just how good fresh gomashio tastes. I keep a batch in the fridge, to sprinkle as a condiment over rice dishes, soups, dumplings — and even home-made sausage rolls and popcorn.

1⅔ cups (250 g) white or black
   sesame seeds
¾ teaspoon sea salt

Put the sesame seeds in a large cold frying pan over medium heat. Cook, stirring and shaking the pan regularly, for 6–8 minutes, or until the seeds are evenly golden.

Transfer the seeds and salt to a food processor or blender and pulse until coarsely chopped.

Transfer the mixture to an airtight jar and store in the fridge; it will stay fresh for up to 3 months... if there is any left by then!

- Great source of vitamin E
- Very low in saturated fat

VEGAN • DAIRY FREE • NUT FREE • EGG FREE

SPELT ROTI Makes 8

Malaysian-style roti is one of my all-time favourite breads. It's normally made with refined wheat flour, submerged in lots of ghee, and then cooked in a lot of ghee. This version is softer and breaks apart more easily because of the spelt flour, but it's still a keeper, especially for boosting your wholegrain intake. Spelt flour is also easier on the gut and digestion, too.

1⅔ cups (225 g) spelt flour
½ teaspoon sea salt
2 tablespoons coconut oil
½ cup (125 ml) coconut milk
neutral-flavoured oil, such as
    rice bran or pure vegetable oil,
    to cover the dough

Combine the flour and salt in a bowl. Using your fingertips, rub the coconut oil into the flour until combined. Make a well in the centre and pour in the coconut milk. Begin to work the milk into the flour mixture with your hands, then knead for about 5 minutes, or until smooth and elastic. Alternatively, you can combine the dough using an electric stand mixer.

Divide the dough into eight equal portions and roll into balls. Place the balls in a small bowl and pour enough oil over to cover; it's okay if the balls are overlapping and squash into each other slightly. Cover with a plate and leave on the bench overnight.

Heat a frying pan over medium heat. Remove one ball at a time from the oil and place on a clean work surface. Using the palm of your hand, begin to flatten the dough out into a circle, until it is about 2 mm (¹/₁₆ inch) thick; you can gently pull the dough from the edges to pull it out further and make it thinner. You can either leave it as one thin round, or fold in the edges to meet in the centre, like an envelope or triangle.

Cook the roti for about 2 minutes on each side, cooking each side for 1 minute at a time, until golden in patches and cooked through. Remove from the pan and quickly (as it's hot!) scrunch up the roti into a ball.

You can keep the roti warm in the oven while cooking the remaining roti. They are best served warm.

LOW CARB

+
1 serve wholegrains per serve

MAKE AHEAD
After rolling the roti out, you can freeze them between sheets of baking paper for up to 3 months. If making them to freeze, keep them round when rolling. Thaw in the fridge overnight before cooking.

VEGETARIAN • DAIRY FREE • VEGAN-ABLE • EGG FREEABLE

MILK BUNS Makes 8

Milk buns are all the craze, unless of course you don't eat dairy. I've made these ones dairy free so no one misses out. You can make them vegan by not brushing them with the egg yolk before baking — although the sesame seeds will fall off very easily!

140 ml (4½ fl oz) tin coconut milk

3 tablespoons extra virgin olive oil,
  plus extra for greasing

1 teaspoon fine sea salt

2 teaspoons instant dried yeast

3 cups (450 g) plain flour

1 egg yolk, beaten, for brushing

sesame seeds, for sprinkling

Combine the coconut milk, oil, salt and ¾ cup (185 ml) water in a small saucepan. Warm over low heat for 1–2 minutes, or until lukewarm.

Combine the yeast and flour in a large bowl and make a well in the centre. Pour the cream mixture into the well and start to work the wet mixture into the dry mixture until combined. Knead on a clean work surface for 5 minutes, or until smooth and elastic.

Lightly grease the bowl, then add the dough and cover with a tea towel. Set aside to prove in a warm, draught-free place for 1 hour, or until doubled in size.

Line a large baking tray with baking paper. Punch down the dough and knead for 2 minutes, then divide into eight portions. Roll into balls and place at least 5 cm (2 inches) apart on the baking tray. Cover with a tea towel and set aside to prove for a further 30 minutes, or until almost doubled in size.

Preheat the oven to 180°C (350°F). Lightly brush the rolls with the egg yolk, then sprinkle with sesame seeds. Place the tray in the oven and reduce the oven temperature to 160°C (315°F).

Bake for 25 minutes, or until the rolls are golden and cooked, and sound hollow when gently tapped on the base.

Allow to cool for 15 minutes before cutting open.

HEALTHY FATS

MAKE AHEAD
Wrap the cooked buns well and freeze for
up to 6 months.

MY SHORTCRUST PASTRY

Makes 1 × 24 cm (9½ inch) tart, about 3 cm (1¼ inches) deep

**3/4
SERVES VEG
per serve**

A vegan shortcrust pastry made with chickpeas? Sounds outrageous, but yes I've found a way to add vegies — in this case, legumes — even to pastry. There are definitely no vegies to be found in a commercial shortcrust, but with half the carbs, and nearly triple the fibre, this vegan version is also lower in calories and a good source of protein. On top of all this, it's easy to make, too.

400 g (14 oz) tin chickpeas, drained;
reserve the aquafaba for making
Mayo (page 192) or Tropical pavlova
(page 185)
4 tablespoons coconut oil
½ teaspoon sea salt
½ cup (75 g) plain flour

Process or blend the chickpeas, oil and salt until smooth. Add the flour and pulse to combine. Turn out onto a clean work surface and bring together into a smooth ball. Shape into a disc and cover with plastic wrap.

At this point you can rest the pastry in the fridge for 20 minutes (or until needed) — or you can roll the pastry out and then rest it in the fridge once you've lined your pie dish.

The pastry will be very firm when you remove it from the fridge, but as it warms up it will also be very soft, so you'll need to work quickly once it has had a few minutes to soften.

Once I've lined the pie dish, I like to rest the pastry again in the fridge or freezer for a further 10–15 minutes while the oven preheats.

Don't be discouraged if the pastry shrinks a little during cooking. Given that it is made using chickpeas, it doesn't behave exactly like a normal shortcrust.

TOP TIP
• Instead of coconut oil, you can use 80 g (2¾ oz) butter; make sure the butter is very cold.

½ serve protein + ¾ serve legumes per serve

MAKE AHEAD
You can make the pastry ahead of time and shape it into a disc. Wrap it well and store for up to 5 days in the fridge, or 6 months in the freezer.

PIZZA DOUGH
Makes 1 large pizza, or 2 smaller ones | Serves 4–6

Adding a serve of veg to a pizza dough in the form of chickpeas might seem a little random, but it's certainly a good way to 'health up' what is typically a 'junk' food. Also, the chickpeas are easily masked by everything else that's going on — and add a source of calcium and protein to the dough that wouldn't otherwise be there.

1
SERVE VEG
per serve

400 g (14 oz) tin chickpeas, drained; reserve the aquafaba for making Mayo (page 192) or Tropical pavlova (page 185)

2 tablespoons extra virgin olive oil, plus extra for greasing

½ teaspoon fine sea salt

1 cup (150 g) wholemeal plain flour

2 teaspoons instant dried yeast

½ teaspoon sugar

Using a food processor, blend the chickpeas, oil and salt together until smooth.

Add the flour, yeast, sugar and ½ cup (125 ml) lukewarm water and pulse to combine.

Turn the dough out onto a clean work surface and knead for 5 minutes, or until smooth and elastic.

Transfer to a greased bowl, cover with a tea towel and set aside in a warm draught-free place to prove for 1 hour, or until doubled in size.

Preheat the oven to 250°C (500°F).

Turn the dough out onto a lightly floured work surface. I like to hand stretch the dough and push it out with my fingertips as thinly as possible without breaking, so it is about 6 mm (¼ inch) thick, but you can also roll the dough out using a rolling pin. I usually shape the dough into one large 35 cm (14 inch) round or rectangle, or you could divide the dough in half and make two smaller pizza bases.

Spread with your favourite pizza sauce and toppings and bake for 15 minutes.

✚
Good source of fibre

MAKE AHEAD
If you wanted to make the dough in advance, you can store it in the fridge overnight once you've kneaded it all together. The temperature of the fridge will slow down the proving process.

PIZZA SAUCE Makes about 300 ml (10½ fl oz)

I find commercial pizza sauces are usually rich and sickly, and often don't taste that great. Try making your own, particularly using home-made passata, and there's really no comparison — except, perhaps, for the ones you'll find in Italy. This simple pizza sauce is quick to prepare, and keeps well in the pantry, so why not make a few extra batches to stash away? Making your own passata (page 207), tomato ketchup (page 226) and stocks (pages 216, 220, 222 and 224) works out to be far more economical, as well as better for you.

1
SERVE VEG
per serve

400 ml (14 fl oz) Roasted tomato passata (page 207), or store-bought tomato passata (puréed tomatoes)
2–3 tablespoons torn basil or oregano
3 tablespoons tomato paste (concentrated purée)

Combine the ingredients in a small saucepan. Cook over medium–low heat for 12–15 minutes, stirring regularly, until thickened.

Leave to cool slightly before using, or pour the hot sauce into a warm sterilised jar with an airtight lid and seal. Turn the jar upside down on a heatproof surface and leave to cool.

The sauce will keep in a cool, dark place for up to 3 months. Once opened, keep in the fridge and use within 1 week, or freeze for up to 6 months.

ROASTED TOMATO PASSATA Makes about 8 cups (2 litres)

There is no simpler fresh tomato sauce than this. There's no peeling of tomato skins (which also means extra fibre) — you just let the oven do all the work, then blend it all together. So versatile, so useful, and full of antioxidants and antibacterial properties, this sauce has a lot going for it. It's also a great one to make at the end of summer when there's an oversupply of tomatoes, or whenever they are on special. Any very ripe tomatoes are fine, although I like to use roma tomatoes as they have fewer seeds.

3/4
SERVES VEG
per serve

2 kg (4 lb 8 oz) very ripe roma
   tomatoes
1 red onion, unpeeled, halved
4 unpeeled garlic cloves
½ cup (125 ml) extra virgin olive oil
2 teaspoons sea salt

Preheat the oven to 200°C (400°F).

Spread the tomatoes, onion and garlic cloves in a large deep baking tray. Drizzle with 2 tablespoons of the oil, sprinkle with the salt, season with freshly ground black pepper and toss to combine.

Roast for 40 minutes, or until the tomato skins have burst and are browned in bits. Remove from the oven and leave to cool.

Discard the onion skins, and squeeze the garlic cloves out of their skins.

Using a food processor or blender, in batches if necessary, blend the tomatoes, onion and garlic (including any liquid in the baking tray) with the remaining 4 tablespoons oil until smooth.

Pour the hot sauce into warm sterilised jars with airtight lids and seal. Turn the jars upside down on a heatproof surface and leave to cool.

The passata will keep in a cool, dark place for up to 3 months. Once opened, keep in the fridge and use within 1 week, or freeze for up to 6 months.

TOP TIP

• To make a **QUICK CHEAT'S PASSATA**, finely chop 1 small red onion and 1 garlic clove and place in a saucepan with 700 ml (24 fl oz) store-bought tomato passata and 2 tablespoons extra virgin olive oil. Season with sea salt, freshly ground black pepper and a large pinch of sugar, then purée using a stick blender. Cover and cook over low heat for 15 minutes, stirring occasionally, until the flavours have infused.

VEGAN • DAIRY FREE • GLUTEN FREE • NUT FREE • EGG FREE

PEPPERINI Makes about 1–2 cups | Serves 4

Move over pepperoni. Although it's fine to enjoy real pepperoni every now and then, we really don't need to be feeding our children (or ourselves!) such highly processed meats, so I prefer not to introduce it into the diet in the first place — hence the creation of 'pepperini'. Made with thin 'coins' of deliciously spiced zucchini, pepperini is full of flavour, and a great substitute for pepperoni as a pizza topping. And there's no warning from the Cancer Council attached.

1/2 SERVE VEG per serve

2 tablespoons extra virgin olive oil
½ teaspoon dried chilli flakes
1½ teaspoons smoked paprika
½ teaspoon garlic powder
1 teaspoon dried oregano
½ teaspoon fennel seeds
1–2 zucchini (courgettes), thinly sliced

Add the oil and spices to a cold, large frying pan and place over medium–low heat. Season with sea salt and freshly ground black pepper. Once the oil is hot, add the zucchini and cook for 3 minutes, stirring regularly, until just tender.

The pepperini is best used fresh, but can be stored in an airtight container in the fridge for up to 5 days. Gently reheat for serving.

TOP TIP

• Instead of zucchini, you can also make this dish using eggplant (aubergine). Just halve 1 small eggplant lengthways and thinly slice. Add an extra 1 tablespoon oil with the spices, salt and pepper. Cook the eggplant for 6–8 minutes, turning regularly, until tender; you may need to add 2 tablespoons water at a time to speed up the cooking process.

HEALTHY FATS
LOW SATURATED FAT
LOW CARB

BOLOGNESE SAUCE Serves 4–6

Legumes make a sneak appearance in this classic sauce, conferring added health benefits. You can easily tailor the sauce to suit the dish you are serving it with and the preferences of your diners. Instead of dried lentils, you could use a 400 g (14 oz) tin of canned lentils, in which case you will not need to use any stock, as the lentils are already cooked; simply rinse and drain the lentils, and stir them in right towards the end just to heat them through, after the sauce has finished simmering.

**3¹/₂
SERVES VEG
per serve**

2 tablespoons olive oil

250 g (9 oz) minced beef or lamb, or a mix of pork and veal

4 anchovy fillets (optional), finely chopped

250 g (9 oz) mushrooms, finely chopped

2 celery stalks, finely chopped

1 carrot, scrubbed, then coarsely grated

⅔ cup (100 g) sun-dried tomatoes, finely chopped

400 ml (14 fl oz) Roasted tomato passata (page 207), or store-bought tomato passata (puréed tomatoes)

½ cup (100 g) dried puy or French-style lentils

2 cups (500 ml) stock of your choice (if using dried lentils; see tips)

Heat 1 tablespoon of the oil in a large deep frying pan or shallow saucepan over high heat; if using minced lamb, there is no need to add any oil. Cook the minced meat for 3 minutes, or until browned. Transfer to a bowl, then drain off and discard any excess liquid.

Reduce the heat to medium–high and heat the remaining oil in the pan. Add the anchovies, if using. Add the mushrooms, celery and carrot and cook for 3–5 minutes, stirring regularly, until starting to soften.

Return the meat to the pan, then stir in the sun-dried tomatoes and passata. Add the dried lentils, along with the stock.

Cover with a lid and bring to a simmer, then reduce the heat to low and cook for 1 hour, or until the mixture has thickened, the meat has broken down and the vegetables are very tender.

Remove the lid. (If using tinned lentils, stir them in now.) Cook, uncovered, for a further 5 minutes, or until the sauce has thickened. Use as required.

TOP TIPS

- If using dried lentils, take care not to season the bolognese with salt until after they are completely cooked, otherwise they will toughen up and will not soften.
- To make a **VEGAN MUSHROOM BOLOGNESE**, omit the meat and anchovies, and use 750 g (1 lb 9 oz) mushrooms in total. Fry them with the celery and carrot, and cook the sauce for 45 minutes, rather than 1 hour. If using dried lentils, use the Mushroom stock on page 216.
- For a quick stock, soak 2 dried shiitake mushrooms in 2 cups (500 ml) boiling water for 15 minutes, then use this liquid as your stock. Discard the woody stems from the rehydrated mushrooms, then add them to the bolognese with the stock, for added texture and flavour.

DIVIDE AND CONQUER

- You can make the entire sauce vegan; then, for those who would like beef, stir the braised beef from the stock on page 224 into their serves, right towards the end to heat through.

- 1 serve protein + 1 serve legumes per serve
- Good source of zinc, vitamin A and potassium

MAKE AHEAD
Store the sauce in an airtight container in the fridge for up to 3 days, or freeze for up to 3 months.

VIETNAMESE PICKLES
Makes enough for 2 × 2 cup (500 ml) jars

These pickles can be found in various shapes and sizes at Vietnamese supermarkets, but they are just so easy to prepare at home and make a delicious topping for salads and dishes such as the banh mi on page 82. My daughter eats them on their own as a snack!

1½ cups (375 ml) white vinegar

3 teaspoons fine sea salt

4 tablespoons sugar

½ small daikon (300 g/10½ oz), peeled and shredded

2 large carrots, scrubbed or peeled, then shredded

2 tablespoons finely chopped coriander (cilantro) stems (optional)

Bring the vinegar, salt, sugar and ¾ cup (185 ml) water to the boil in a small saucepan.

Meanwhile, put the daikon, carrot and coriander, if using, into two sterilised 2 cup (500 ml) jars.

Pour the hot pickling liquid over the vegetables to cover. Seal the jars and leave to cool.

The pickles will keep in the fridge for up to 1 month.

TOP TIPS

- A julienne peeler is the perfect little kitchen tool that makes shredding vegetables quick and simple, with minimal washing up. These gadgets are inexpensive and handy for small kitchens as they don't take up any space.
- The pickles need to steep for at least 1 hour before using.

CREAMED CORN Makes about 3 cups (650 g)

2¹/₂
SERVES VEG
per serve

Home-made creamed corn tastes so much fresher than the tinned stuff, and is so quick and simple to prepare — plus it's lower in salt, and doesn't contain any added sugars. It makes a nutritious side dish, and I also use it in recipes such as Corn fritters (page 14) and Corn dogs (page 31). The cooking time will depend on whether you're using fresh or frozen corn. Fresh kernels will take longer to cook, and if using frozen kernels, you may not need to add any extra water when blending.

1 tablespoon butter or extra virgin olive oil (or a combination)

2 garlic cloves, finely chopped

1 onion, finely chopped

500 g (1 lb 2 oz) fresh or frozen corn kernels

2 teaspoons white wine vinegar

Heat the butter in a small saucepan over medium heat. Sauté the garlic and onion for 3 minutes, or until lightly golden, stirring regularly.

Stir in the corn, vinegar and ½ cup (125 ml) water. Cover and cook for a further 5–10 minutes, or until the corn is softened and cooked.

Season to taste with sea salt and freshly ground black pepper. Add 3 tablespoons water and purée using a stick blender until smooth.

Gently reheat for serving, or refrigerate or freeze until required.

TOP TIP

- You can use this recipe to make **MUSHY PEAS**, using 500 g (1 lb 2 oz) fresh or frozen peas. The method and other ingredients are exactly the same. Fresh peas will take a little longer to cook, and if using frozen peas, you may not need to add any extra water when blending.

- To make the recipe vegan or dairy free, use olive oil instead of butter.

MAKE AHEAD

Store in an airtight container in the fridge for up to 3 days, or freeze for up to 6 months. You can easily make up a couple of batches to keep in the freezer. It's so delicious it will never go to waste.

SWEET CREAMED CORN Makes about 1 cup (250 g)

**1
SERVE VEG
per serve**

Here's a sweeter version of the Creamed corn recipe on page 213, which I use in desserts. Taking advantage of the natural sweetness of corn means you won't need to be adding too much sugar to sweeter dishes.

1½ tablespoons butter or olive oil
2 teaspoons vanilla bean paste or
    natural vanilla extract
1¼ cups (250 g) fresh corn kernels, or
    1⅔ cups (250 g) frozen corn kernels
a pinch of sea salt

Heat the butter in a saucepan over medium heat. Add the remaining ingredients and 3–4 tablespoons water and cover with a lid. Cook for 3–5 minutes, or until the kernels have softened and are warmed through.

If using fresh corn, add 3 tablespoons water to the pan; if using frozen kernels, you may not need to add any extra water at this point, as they contain more water to begin with. Using a stick blender, purée the mixture until smooth.

Use as required, or refrigerate or freeze until required.

TOP TIP
• **To make the recipe vegan or dairy free, use olive oil instead of butter.**

✚
No added sugars

MAKE AHEAD
Store in an airtight container in the fridge for up to 5 days, or freeze for up to 6 months. You can easily make up a few batches to keep in the freezer.

VEGAN • DAIRY FREE • GLUTEN FREE • NUT FREE • EGG FREE

MUSHROOM STOCK Makes 6–8 cups (1.5–2 litres)

Adding shiitake mushrooms to any stock gives a lovely richness and umami savouriness to the finished dish, often unmatched by other vegetables. It's definitely worth investing in a packet of dried shiitake, as they are very reasonably priced and will keep for ages. I use this stock as my all-round vegetable stock, but if you would like to add other vegetables to contribute other flavours, by all means go for it. On occasion, I also add carrots and celery — and even fresh corn cobs (without the kernels), which impart a lovely sweetness.

8 dried shiitake mushrooms
6 spring onions (scallions), trimmed
  and coarsely chopped
4 garlic cloves, peeled
2 teaspoons fine sea salt

Soak the mushrooms in 4 cups (1 litre) warm water for at least 4 hours, or even overnight.

Using a stick blender or food processor, finely chop the spring onions and garlic, then add them to a large saucepan with any juices from the chopping (see tip). Add the soaked mushrooms and the mushroom soaking water. Add the salt and an additional 12 cups (3 litres) water.

Bring to a simmer over medium–high heat, then reduce the heat to medium and simmer for 1 hour, or until the stock has reduced by about half and the flavour has developed.

Drain the stock through a fine sieve, set inside a large bowl or saucepan. Discard the solids.

The stock will keep in an airtight container in the fridge for up to 5 days, or in the freezer for up to 6 months.

TOP TIP

- It may seem like an unnecessary messing up of equipment, but whizzing the spring onions and garlic using a stick blender or food processor releases the juices from them, adding an extra level of flavour that you don't get from chopping.

MUSHROOM GRAVY Serves 4

This is one gutsy gravy, which is why I've suggested it as a very credible substitute to a chicken or beef gravy in other recipes in the book. To keep this recipe quick, I've left the dried shiitake mushrooms whole. If you have a bit of time, you could soak the dried shiitake for a good hour or so, until completely softened, then very finely slice them and keep them in the gravy for extra texture. The gravy freezes well, so it's worth making an extra batch or two while you're at it.

4 dried shiitake mushrooms
2 tablespoons butter
1 tablespoon olive oil
200 g (7 oz) fresh mushrooms of your
  choice, cleaned and thinly sliced
2 garlic cloves, finely chopped
1 tablespoon gluten-free or plain flour
1 tablespoon cornflour

Soak the shiitake mushrooms in 4 cups (1 litre) boiling water for at least 10 minutes while you prepare the other ingredients, or up to 30 minutes if you have the time. Discard the woody stems.

Melt the butter in a wide shallow saucepan or deep frying pan over medium heat, swirling the pan until the butter turns golden and has a nutty aroma. Add the oil and sliced fresh mushrooms and cook for 5 minutes, stirring regularly. Add the garlic and cook for a further minute.

Stir in the flour and cornflour and allow to cook out for 1 minute. Gradually stir in the soaking liquid from the shiitake mushrooms, along with the shiitake mushrooms. Bring to a simmer and cook for 10 minutes, or until the gravy has thickened slightly. Remove the whole shiitake mushrooms and season to taste with sea salt and freshly ground black pepper.

The gravy will keep in an airtight container in the fridge for up to 3 days, or in the freezer for up to 6 months. Gently reheat for serving.

TOP TIPS

- You can add 1 tablespoon finely chopped sage (or another favourite herb) to the gravy. If using rosemary, I would only start with 1 teaspoon finely chopped (depending on the dish you're using the gravy with), as it can be rather overpowering.
- To make the gravy vegan or dairy free, use olive oil instead of butter.
- For a gluten-free gravy, use gluten-free flour and cornflour.

ROASTED POTATO MASH Serves 4

We're all used to peeling and boiling potatoes, throwing away all of the nutrients in the skin, as well as those that have leached into the water during cooking. I find that keeping the skin on the potatoes gives the mash a pleasant texture, and cuts down on preparation time, too.

**2¹/₂
SERVES VEG
per serve**

800 g (1 lb 12 oz) starchy/floury
    potatoes or sweet potatoes,
    scrubbed well, cut into 2 cm
    (¾ inch) chunks
olive oil, for drizzling
3 tablespoons butter or extra virgin
    olive oil or (or a combination)

Preheat the oven to 220°C (425°F). Line a large baking tray with baking paper.

Spread the potatoes out on the tray, drizzle with olive oil and season with sea salt, tossing to combine. Cover with foil, then roast on the highest shelf of the oven for 10 minutes.

Remove the foil and bake for a further 10–15 minutes, or until tender.

Transfer the potatoes to a saucepan and place over low heat with the butter. Mash and season to taste with sea salt and freshly ground black pepper.

Serve immediately, or keep warm over low heat.

TOP TIPS

- You can really jazz up your mash and get creative by using other vegetables, such as pumpkin, parsnips or celeriac, or even a combination. Just be aware that other root vegetables can cook at different rates, and when mixed together, some may end up a strange colour!
- Try also adding some chopped parsley or chives to your mash, or your favourite herb.
- To make the mash vegan or dairy free, use olive oil instead of butter.

DAIRY FREEABLE • GLUTEN FREE • NUT FREE • EGG FREE

CHICKEN STUFFING Makes around 400 g (14 oz)

This is what you call 'chicken stuffing'! It has all the flavours of a conventional bread-based chicken stuffing, but without the bread. Here, the chicken is a complementary component to the *real* heroes of our food: vegetables. Use this 'chicken stuffing' to stuff the sweet potatoes on page 132, the Chick-in schnitzels on page 152, or as a topper on salads. You can even use it instead of pork in the roast dinner on page 135, complete with gravy, or instead of lamb in the Toad in the hole on page 121. It's also great with the poutine on page 93 — and I'm sure you'll also find many other tasty uses for it, too.

30 g (1 oz) butter
1 red onion, finely chopped
2 garlic cloves, finely chopped
350 g (12 oz) shredded cooked
    chicken, such as tenderloin or breast,
    or from a good-quality barbecued
    chicken
1 tablespoon finely chopped sage
    or thyme, or 1 teaspoon rosemary
2 tablespoons finely chopped parsley
finely grated zest of 1 lemon
2 teaspoons dijon or wholegrain
    mustard

Melt the butter in a frying pan over medium heat. Sauté the onion and garlic for 5 minutes, or until golden.

Stir in the remaining ingredients until well combined. Season to taste with sea salt and freshly ground black pepper.

Use straight away, or store in an airtight container in the fridge for up to 3 days, or in the freezer for up to 3 months.

TOP TIPS
- You can reheat the stuffing in a saucepan over medium–low heat, with 1–2 tablespoons stock or water to keep it moist.
- To make the stuffing dairy free, use olive oil instead of butter.

MAKE AHEAD
If you have excess chicken, it's so easy to make up
a double or triple batch to keep in the freezer.

DAIRY FREE • GLUTEN FREE • NUT FREE • EGG FREE

CHICKEN STOCK Makes 6–8 cups (1.5–2 litres)

Store-bought stocks are really convenient, but it bothers me that their base flavours don't suit all cuisines, particularly Asian ones, and I also find that Asian-style stocks contain flavour enhancers. With this in mind, I have created this stock to be used interchangeably across all sorts of cuisines — and you can feel comfortable about what's in it, too. Using good-quality bones is just as important as using good-quality meat, so whenever I'm making stock I always pick up some organic bones from my local organic supermarket.

1 tablespoon olive oil
1 organic chicken carcass, or 500 g
   (1 lb 2 oz) organic chicken wings
6 spring onions (scallions), trimmed
   and coarsely chopped
4 dried shiitake mushrooms

Heat the oil in a large saucepan over medium–high heat. Cook the chicken for 6–8 minutes, turning regularly, until golden. Season with sea salt.

Using a stick blender or food processor (see tip), finely chop the spring onions and add them to the saucepan with the dried mushrooms and 16 cups (4 litres) water.

Bring to a simmer over medium–high heat, then reduce the heat to medium and simmer for 1¼ hours, skimming any scum from the surface.

Strain out the solids, reserving the shiitake mushrooms for the Chicken gravy (see opposite page).

The stock will keep in an airtight container in the fridge for up to 3 days, or in the freezer for up to 6 months.

TOP TIPS

- You could also poach a chicken breast in the stock, to use in other recipes. Add it during the last 15 minutes or so of simmering for maximum flavour, reduce the heat to low and cover with a lid. Set the timer to 12 minutes for a 180 g (6 oz) chicken breast, or 15 minutes for a 250 g (9 oz) chicken breast. When the timer goes off, remove the chicken breast from the stock. Set aside to cool before shredding and using in other recipes.
- It may seem an unnecessary use of equipment, but whizzing the spring onions using a stick blender or food processor releases the juices from the spring onions that you don't get from chopping, adding extra flavour to the stock.

DAIRY FREEABLE • GLUTEN FREEABLE • NUT FREE • EGG FREE

CHICKEN GRAVY Serves 4

This chicken gravy is probably much lighter in feel and colour than you may be used to. It's surprising just how many ingredients, including colours and thickeners, are added to some chicken gravies. With this one, there's no need to feel terrible about a big pour of gravy onto your plate.

30 g (1 oz) butter

1 tablespoon extra virgin olive oil

1 tablespoon gluten-free or plain flour

1 tablespoon cornflour

4 cups (1 litre) Chicken stock (see opposite page), or use a good-quality store-bought chicken stock

4 rehydrated shiitake mushrooms, reserved from the Chicken stock (opposite page)

Melt the butter in a wide shallow saucepan or deep frying pan over medium heat, swirling the pan until the butter turns golden and has a nutty aroma.

Stir in the oil, flour and cornflour and cook for 1 minute, stirring regularly. Gradually stir in the stock and mushrooms, stirring vigorously to avoid lumps; you can use a whisk at this stage if you prefer.

Bring to a simmer and cook for 10–15 minutes, or until the gravy has thickened slightly. Season to taste with sea salt and freshly ground black pepper. Strain out the solids before using.

The gravy will keep in an airtight container in the fridge for up to 3 days, or in the freezer for up to 6 months.

TOP TIPS

- To make the gravy vegan or dairy free, use olive oil instead of butter.
- For a gluten-free gravy, use gluten-free flour and cornflour.
- if using a store-bought chicken stock, use one with minimal added salt, or your gravy may end up overly salty.

LAMB STOCK Makes 6–8 cups (1.5–2 litres)

You can't buy lamb stock, or not very readily anyway, so here's the perfect way to braise lamb shanks and make lamb stock at the same time. Try using the lamb stock in place of beef stock for a subtle flavour change. The braised lamb is lovely in a pie, and can be used instead of the chicken in the chicken and vegetable pie on page 122, or instead of the beef in the Steak and kidney bean pie on page 124. The Apple sauce from page 196 would go well with the braised lamb, too.

2 lamb shanks
500 g (1 lb 2 oz) good-quality lamb
    bones
1 tablespoon olive oil
2 carrots, coarsely chopped
2 celery stalks, coarsely chopped
1 brown or red onion, coarsely chopped
2 garlic cloves, coarsely chopped
2 dried shiitake mushrooms (optional)
parsley sprigs (optional)

Season the lamb shanks and bones with sea salt. Heat the oil in a large saucepan over high heat. Add the bones and shanks and cook for 5 minutes, or until well browned, turning now and then.

Add the remaining ingredients, and enough water to cover.

Bring to the boil, skimming the scum from the surface, then reduce the heat to low and cover with a lid. Cook for 30 minutes.

Remove the lid and increase the heat to a gentle simmer. Continue to cook for a further 1 hour, or until the lamb on the shanks is tender and falling apart, topping up with more water to keep the ingredients fully submerged.

Remove the shanks from the pan and set aside until cool. Shred the meat to use in other recipes.

Strain out the solids, reserving any shiitake mushrooms for the Lamb gravy (see opposite page).

The stock and the braised lamb will keep in an airtight container in the fridge for up to 3 days, or in the freezer for up to 6 months.

DAIRY FREE • GLUTEN FREEABLE • NUT FREE • EGG FREE

LAMB GRAVY Serves 4

As the lamb stock is rather light in flavour as far as stocks go, this gravy isn't
too rich, either — but you can easily use it instead of chicken or beef gravy.
Try pairing this gravy with the braised lamb from the Lamb stock (opposite)
in place of the pork in the Quick 'roast' pork dinner on page 135.

2 tablespoons olive oil
4 rehydrated shiitake mushrooms,
  reserved from the Lamb stock
  (see opposite page)
1 tablespoon gluten-free or plain flour
1 tablespoon cornflour
4 cups (1 litre) Lamb stock (see
  opposite page); remove the fat layer
  from the top
½–1 teaspoon finely chopped rosemary
  (optional, see tip)

Add the oil and mushrooms to a saucepan and place over medium heat. Once
hot, stir in the flour and cornflour and cook for 1 minute, stirring constantly.
Gradually stir in the stock and rosemary.

Bring to a simmer and cook for 10 minutes, or until the gravy has thickened
slightly. Season to taste with sea salt and freshly ground black pepper. Strain out
any solids before using.

The gravy will keep in an airtight container in the fridge for up to 3 days,
or in the freezer for up to 6 months.

TOP TIP
• If you'd like to add rosemary to the gravy, it is best to start with a lesser
  amount, as it can impart a bitterness to the gravy if too much is added.
• For a gluten-free gravy, use gluten-free flour and cornflour.

BEEF STOCK Makes 6–8 cups (1.5–2 litres)

When making beef stock, which is also the base of the beef gravy opposite, I like to braise a bit of beef at the same time, to use in other recipes such as the Steak and kidney bean pie on page 124. You can make this stock without the beef if you prefer, but I think it's a great way to cook a few things at once. So streamlined, so easy. Why not make a double batch of the stock and beef, which you can freeze separately for up to 3 months to use later on? If a good-quality piece of meat is on special, this is also a good opportunity to batch-cook.

400 g (14 oz) chuck steak, cut in half
500 g (1 lb 2 oz) good-quality beef
  bones
1 tablespoon olive oil
2 carrots, coarsely chopped
2 celery stalks, coarsely chopped
1 brown or red onion, coarsely chopped
2 garlic cloves, coarsely chopped
4 dried shiitake mushrooms (optional)

Season the beef and bones with sea salt. Heat the oil in a large saucepan over high heat. Add the bones and beef and cook for 5 minutes, or until well browned, turning now and then.

Add the remaining ingredients and 12–16 cups (3–4 litres) water and bring to the boil, skimming the scum from the surface.

Reduce the heat to a gentle simmer and cook for 2 hours, or until the beef is tender and falling apart. Remove from the pan and set aside until cool.

Strain out the solids, reserving any shiitake mushrooms for the Beef gravy (see opposite page).

Once cool enough to handle, shred the beef into large chunks and transfer to an airtight container. Drizzle with 1–2 tablespoons of the stock to stop it drying out. The beef will keep in the fridge for 2–3 days, or in the freezer for up to 3 months.

The stock will keep in an airtight container in the fridge for up to 3 days, or in the freezer for up to 6 months.

TOP TIPS

• When braising 400 g (14 oz) beef chuck, you'll end up with about 280 g (10 oz). You can shred the beef and use it in recipes such as the Tasty taco salad on page 113, or use it with a Bolognese sauce (page 210) to replace minced beef. Try it with the poutine (page 93) instead of the chicken stuffing, in the Chicken and veg pie 'til you die (page 122) instead of chicken, or even in the Toad in the hole (page 121) instead of lamb.

BEEF GRAVY Serves 4

There is nothing quite as 'meaty' as a beef gravy. This 'minimal meat' gravy isn't too rich, but is still very flavoursome, so it is a great accompaniment to dishes if you are trying to cut down on your meat consumption.

30 g (1 oz) butter

1 tablespoon extra virgin olive oil

2 dried shiitake mushrooms, reserved from the Beef stock opposite (optional)

2 teaspoons thyme leaves (optional)

1 tablespoon gluten-free or plain flour

1 tablespoon cornflour

4 cups (1 litre) Beef stock (see opposite page)

1 teaspoon fine sea salt

Melt the butter in a saucepan over medium heat, swirling the pan for 2–3 minutes, or until the butter turns golden and has a nutty aroma.

Add the oil, and if using the mushrooms and thyme, add these as well. Stir in the flour and cornflour and cook for 1 minute, stirring constantly to cook out the raw flour taste.

Gradually whisk in the stock. Bring to a simmer and cook for 10 minutes, or until the gravy has thickened slightly. Season with the salt, and freshly ground black pepper to taste. Strain out any solids before using.

The gravy will keep in an airtight container in the fridge for up to 3 days, or in the freezer for up to 6 months.

TOP TIPS

- You can add herbs, such as rosemary or oregano, to suit the dish you are serving the gravy with.
- To make the gravy dairy free, use olive oil instead of butter.
- For a gluten-free gravy, use gluten-free flour and cornflour.

VEGAN • DAIRY FREE • GLUTEN FREE • NUT FREE • EGG FREE

CHUNKY TOMATO KETCHUP

Makes approximately 600 ml (21 fl oz)

A major difference between this and your everyday ketchup is that the commercial version has ten times as much sugar! This is my happy medium between a tomato relish, and a tomato sauce or ketchup. It's super easy to prepare and tastes remarkably like tomato ketchup, though in consistency it's more like a chutney or pickled tomatoes. Whenever I use this ketchup, I scoop up mostly the tomatoes from the jar; it's normal to have some liquid leftover at the bottom, which you could actually reuse to make more ketchup. I like to use a mixture of tomatoes, of different shapes and sizes.

500 g (1 lb 2 oz) tomatoes, larger ones
   sliced or coarsely chopped
4 tablespoons vinegar, such as red
   wine, white wine or cider vinegar
3 tablespoons maple syrup
2 teaspoons smoked paprika
1 teaspoon sea salt

Preheat the oven to 200°C (400°F).

Combine all the ingredients in a small baking dish, sprinkle with lots of freshly ground black pepper and roast for 30 minutes, or until the tomatoes are very soft and the liquid in the baking dish has thickened slightly.

Transfer the entire mixture to a sterilised jar and seal.

The ketchup will keep in the fridge for up to 3 months; bring to room temperature for serving.

VEGO BALLS
Makes about 20 balls or patties | Serves 4

1¹/₂ SERVES VEG per serve

These balls are softer than your average meatballs, but once in the pan they set and firm up. They won't end up as perfect-looking balls, but more irregular shapes, but I don't think anyone will mind as they're so tasty, not to mention nutritious. Instead of mushrooms, you could use 100 g (3½ oz) baby spinach leaves. Place them in a bowl, pour over enough boiling water to cover, then drain and squeeze out as much liquid as possible. Finely chop before adding to the bean mixture. These vego balls are great to have stashed away in the freezer, making it quick and easy to adapt meals for vegetarian family members and friends.

400 g (14 oz) tin beans, such as borlotti or cannellini beans, drained well

¾ cup (100 g) finely chopped walnuts

100 g (3½ oz) chickpea or buckwheat flour

100 g (scant ½ cup) fresh firm ricotta cheese

1½ cups (150 g) finely chopped mushrooms

1 egg white

½ cup (30 g) coarsely chopped basil or parsley leaves

2 garlic cloves, crushed or finely chopped

½ teaspoon sea salt

2 tablespoons olive oil

Lightly mash the beans in a large bowl using a fork or masher. Add all the remaining ingredients, except the oil. Season with freshly ground black pepper, mixing well with your hands to combine.

Using damp hands, roll the mixture into 4 cm (1½ inch) balls.

Heat the oil in a large frying pan over medium heat. Cook the balls in batches, turning regularly, for 5 minutes, or until browned all over. Remove from the pan and set aside.

Use as required, or store in an airtight container in the fridge for up to 3 days.

(see photo page 228)

**HIGH IN PROTEIN
LOW CARB
HEALTHY FATS
LOW CHOLESTEROL
(14 MG PER SERVE)**

• 1½ serves protein per serve
• No added sugars

MAKE AHEAD
Make a double batch and freeze some for later. Place the vego balls in an airtight container, not touching each other if possible, and store in the freezer for up to 6 months. You can also freeze the mixture whole, then roll into balls after it has thawed in the fridge.

From left to right:

PORK DUMPLING BALLS
(see recipe page 233),

VEGO BALLS
(see recipe page 227)

**BEEF, LAMB, OR VEAL
AND PORK MEATBALLS**
(see recipe page 232)

FISH BALLS
(see recipe page 230)

CHICKEN MEATBALLS
(see recipe page 231)

FISH BALLS Makes about 16 balls or patties | Serves 4

These tasty numbers were inspired by Thai fish cakes and Chinese fish balls — which is why the same basic mixture can be shaped into patties and served like Thai fish cakes, or rolled into balls and served in a soup. Or you can turn them into prawn balls or patties by using 400 g (14 oz) prawn meat instead of the fish — so easy! If you are making these fish or prawn balls to use in the Fish ball laksa on page 148, you could use the leftover broccoli stems from that recipe here instead of (or even as well as) the snake beans or green beans, instead of throwing the broccoli stems away. Peel and finely grate the stems before adding them to the mixture.

1 French shallot, coarsely chopped

1 kaffir lime leaf, finely chopped,
   or 1 tablespoon finely chopped
   coriander (cilantro), Vietnamese mint
   or Thai basil

1 egg white

400 g (14 oz) skinless, boneless firm
   white fish, coarsely chopped

2 tablespoons cornflour

½ teaspoon sea salt

⅔ cup (100 g) finely grated carrot

½ cup (50 g) thinly sliced snake beans
   or green beans

Process the shallot in a food processor until very finely chopped. Add the lime leaf or herbs, egg white, fish, cornflour and salt. Season with ground white or black pepper.

Process for 1 minute to work the mixture together. Add the carrot and snake beans and pulse to combine.

Roll the mixture into 4 cm (1½ inch) balls or patties, and use as required (see tips).

TOP TIPS

- If shaping the mixture into balls, add them to your soup towards the end of cooking time and simmer until just cooked through.
- If shaping the mixture into patties, cook them as you do with the patties in the Fish bowl recipe on page 78. Or make them a snack by frying them off in a pan with a little neutral-flavoured oil over medium–high heat for about 2 minutes each side, or until golden and cooked; they're great with the Tangy Asian dressing on page 195.

(see photo page 229)

MAKE AHEAD

Make a double batch and freeze some for later. (Be sure to use only fresh fish, so you are not refreezing thawed-out fish.) Shape the raw mixture into balls or patties, place a small piece of baking paper between each one (to stop them sticking), place in an airtight container and freeze for up to 3 months.

CHICKEN MEATBALLS

Makes about 24 | Serves 4–6

I've added wholegrain burghul here instead of breadcrumbs, as another great way to boost your daily wholegrain intake. Depending on how fussy your crowd is, pan-frying may be the way to go, because you can disguise the contents of the meatballs a little more easily.

1/2 SERVE VEG per serve

½ cup (100 g) burghul

250–300 g (9–10½ oz) minced chicken

1 zucchini (courgette), coarsely grated, squeezed of as much excess liquid as possible

100 g (3½ oz) feta cheese (optional)

2 garlic cloves, crushed or finely chopped

2 teaspoons dried mint or oregano (or a combination)

1 teaspoon fine sea salt

Put the burghul in a large bowl and cover with 125 ml (½ cup) water. Cover with a plate and set aside for 10 minutes to absorb the liquid.

Fluff the burghul grains with a fork. Add the remaining ingredients and season with freshly ground black pepper. Using your hands, mix for a minute or so until very well combined, then roll into 3–4 cm (1¼–1½ inch) balls.

Use as recipe directs, or transfer to an airtight container and keep in the fridge and use within 2–3 days, depending on the expiry date on your chicken.

TOP TIP

- You can add these meatballs to a simmering soup towards the end of cooking time; they should only take about 5 minutes to cook through.
- To pan-fry them, cook them in a little olive oil over medium–high heat, turning regularly, for about 5 minutes, or until cooked through.
- For dairy-free meatballs, omit the cheese.
- To make the meatballs gluten free, cook ½ cup (100 g) quinoa instead of the burghul.

(see photo page 229)

+
1 serve wholegrains per serve

MAKE AHEAD

Make a double batch and freeze some for later. Place the meatballs in an airtight container, not touching each other if possible, and store in the freezer for up to 3 months. You can also freeze the mixture whole, then roll into balls after it has thawed in the fridge.

BEEF, LAMB, OR VEAL AND PORK MEATBALLS

Makes about 16 | Serves 4

just under 1 SERVE VEG per serve

Boosting your meatballs to the point of having almost 1 serve of veg in every four balls is quite an achievement. If they're served pan-fried on their own, the kids might pick up the other ingredients, but with sauce or gravy over the top, they'll never know! I chop most of the ingredients in a food processor to speed things up.

300 g (10½ oz) lean minced beef or lamb, or a mix of pork and veal

2 cups (200 g) finely grated or finely chopped broccoli

2 garlic cloves, crushed or finely chopped

2 anchovy fillets, finely chopped (optional)

2 spring onions (scallions), finely chopped

2 teaspoons dried Italian herbs

⅓ cup (30 g) finely grated parmesan cheese (optional)

1 egg

½ cup (30 g) fresh breadcrumbs, such as spelt or gluten-free

Combine all the ingredients in a large bowl, mixing well with your hands for 1 minute to work the mixture together and help tenderise the meat.

Roll into 4 cm (1½ inch) balls and use as recipe directs, or transfer to an airtight container, keep in the fridge and use within 2–3 days, depending on the expiry date of the meat.

TOP TIP

- To pan-fry the meatballs, heat 1 tablespoon olive oil in a large deep frying pan over medium heat. Cook the meatballs in batches, turning regularly for 8–10 minutes, or until golden and cooked through.
- For dairy-free meatballs, omit the cheese.
- To make the meatballs gluten free, use gluten-free breadcrumbs.

(see photo pages 228–29)

HIGH IN PROTEIN LOW CARB

✚
Great source of vitamin C and B$_{12}$

MAKE AHEAD
You can make a double batch and freeze some for later. Place the meatballs in an airtight container, not touching each other if possible, and store in the freezer for up to 3 months. You can also freeze the mixture whole, then roll into balls after it has thawed in the fridge.

DAIRY FREE • GLUTEN FREE • NUT FREE • EGG FREE

PORK DUMPLING BALLS

Makes 550 g (1 lb 4 oz) | Serves 4

Rather than being pan-fried on their own, this mixture is best rolled into small balls and used inside dumplings, such as the ones on page 21, or simmered in a soup.

1/2
SERVE VEG
per serve

200 g (7 oz) wombok or savoy
   cabbage, very thinly sliced
½ teaspoon fine sea salt
250 g (9 oz) minced pork
½ cup (50 g) thinly sliced snow peas
   (mangetout)
1 tablespoon finely grated fresh ginger
2 spring onions (scallions), finely
   chopped
2 garlic cloves, crushed or finely
   chopped
2 tablespoons Sesame salt (page 200)
   or toasted sesame seeds
1 tablespoon cornflour
ground white pepper, for seasoning
   (optional)

Put the cabbage in a bowl and sprinkle with the salt. Using your hands, thoroughly massage the salt into the cabbage. Set aside for 15 minutes, then drain and squeeze out the excess moisture.

Add the remaining ingredients to the bowl. Using your hands, mix well for about 1 minute, to work the mixture together and help tenderise the meat.

Use as recipe directs, or transfer to an airtight container, keep in the fridge and use within 2–3 days, depending on the expiry date of the pork.

(see photo page 228)

MAKE AHEAD

Make a double batch and freeze some for later. Place the meatballs in an airtight container, not touching each other if possible, and store in the freezer for up to 3 months. You can also freeze the mixture whole, then roll into balls after it has thawed in the fridge.

CHICKEN LIVER PÂTÉ

Makes 500 g (1 lb 2 oz) | Serves 16 | 1 serve = 50 g (1¾ oz)

It's pretty well known how nutritious liver is, and it seems like pâté is the only palatable way for most people to get their intake. I wanted to make a pâté that wasn't full of cream and butter, so this one is thickened with coconut oil and cashews instead. If you don't have a blender, you can purée the mixture using a hand-held stick blender. And you can easily halve the recipe, if you don't think you'll be able to consume it all within 5 days.

½ cup (80 g) cashews

3 tablespoons coconut oil, plus an extra 3 tablespoons for covering

500 g (1 lb 2 oz) cleaned chicken livers

1 red onion, finely chopped

2 garlic cloves, crushed or finely chopped

2 tablespoons brandy

3 tablespoons extra virgin olive oil

1 teaspoon fine sea salt

½ teaspoon ground white pepper

Soak the cashews in a small bowl of hot water seasoned with a pinch of sea salt for at least 1 hour, until softened. Drain, rinse well and set aside.

Heat 1 tablespoon of the coconut oil in a large frying pan over medium–low heat. Add half the livers and fry for 3 minutes on each side, or until cooked through but not coloured. Remove and set aside. Repeat with the remaining livers and another 1 tablespoon of the coconut oil.

Add the onion and garlic to the pan and cook for 4 minutes, stirring regularly, until golden. Stir in the brandy and cook for 2 minutes, or until the brandy has evaporated. Return the livers to the pan and stir to combine. Remove from the heat and set aside.

Place another 1 tablespoon coconut oil in a blender. Add the olive oil and drained cashews and purée until as smooth as possible. Add the brandied liver mixture from the pan, sprinkle with the salt and pepper, and purée until as smooth as possible.

In batches, push the mixture through a fine sieve, into a bowl, discarding any solids. Transfer to an airtight container.

Gently melt the remaining 3 tablespoons coconut oil and pour it over the surface of the pâté, to completely cover it. The oil layer will solidify in the fridge, and will stop the pâté discolouring and help preserve it.

The pâté will keep in the fridge for up to 5 days.

TOP TIPS

- The longer you soak the cashews, the softer they will be. You can leave them overnight and give them a good rinse before using.
- It's difficult to get the pâté perfectly smooth, so don't worry too much if there are some coarser cashew grains when you're pushing the mixture through the sieve. Straining is also optional.

- 200% RDI vitamin B_{12} per serve
- Over 100% RDI folate per serve

INDEX

THANK YOU

To my husband, Alistair: I am truly grateful for your love and tireless support throughout this journey. Without you, my dream could never have been realised. You kept the wheels turning in our family and home: thank you. Oh, and I cannot forget to mention your impeccable and much appreciated skill for dreaming up witty recipe titles. To my publisher, Jane Morrow: thank you for believing in me and in this project. My dear friends David Morgan and Phu Tang: your incredibly talented minds have done it again. Thank you for having so much 'fun' with this, my dream team. To the wonderful culinary team at Marley Spoon: thank you for picking up the pieces for me at work to allow me the time to write this book. To the extraordinary team at Murdoch Books – Katri, Jane P, Viv, Susanne, and also Northwood Green – I cannot thank you enough. And, lastly, to my true inspiration (and kick-arse food critic), my daughter, Harriet. It's all for you, my darling.

Published in 2019 by Murdoch Books, an imprint of Allen & Unwin

Murdoch Books Australia
83 Alexander Street,
Crows Nest NSW 2065
Phone: +61 (0)2 8425 0100
murdochbooks.com.au
info@murdochbooks.com.au

Murdoch Books UK
Ormond House, 26–27 Boswell Street,
London, WC1N 3JZ
Phone: +44 (0) 20 8785 5995
murdochbooks.co.uk
info@murdochbooks.co.uk

For corporate orders and custom publishing contact our business development team at salesenquiries@murdochbooks.com.au

Publisher: Jane Morrow
Editorial Manager: Jane Price
Editor: Katri Hilden
Design Manager: Vivien Valk
Designer: Susanne Geppert
Photography: Phu Tang
Stylist: David Morgan
Food preparation at shoot: Olivia Andrews, Alistair Clarkson
Nutritionist: Brigit Ambrose
Production Director: Lou Playfair

ISBN 978 1 76063 368 4 Australia
ISBN 978 1 91163 202 3 UK

A cataloguing-in-publication entry is available from the catalogue of the National Library of Australia at nla.gov.au

A catalogue record for this book is available from the British Library
Colour reproduction by Splitting Image Colour Studio Pty Ltd, Clayton, Victoria
Printed by 1010 Printing Co Ltd, China

The author and publisher thank the following for generously supplying ingredients and props during the photography for this book: Harris Farm Markets, Kilner, Chasseur, Avanti, Pyrolux.